Discipline in the
Junior High / Middle School:
A Handbook for Teachers,
Counselors, and Administrators

William E. Stradley

and

Richard D. Aspinall

The Center for Applied Research in Education, Inc.

521 Fifth Avenue

New York, N.Y. 10017

© 1975 by

THE CENTER FOR APPLIED
RESEARCH IN EDUCATION, INC.
NEW YORK, N.Y.

Library of Congress Cataloging in Publication Data

Stradley, William E
    Discipline in the junior high/middle school.

    1. School discipline--Handbooks, manuals, etc.
2. Teacher-student relationships--Handbooks, man-
uals, etc. I. Aspinall, Richard D.
joint author. II. Title.
LB3013.S79   373.1'5   75-8585
ISBN 0-87628-264-8

Printed in the United States of America

About the Authors

William E. Stradley and Richard D. Aspinall have a combined experience as educators of nearly half a century. Presently, they are serving as principal and assistant principal, respectively, of Goddard Middle School, Littleton, Colorado.

Mr. Stradley has been a practicing educator for 26 years. In this time he has served as both teacher and administrator at the elementary, middle, and senior high school levels. During his 16 years as a middle school principal, he has developed a number of effective innovative approaches to middle level education. He has also been active as a consultant, as president of the Colorado Middle Level Executives, as president of the Educational Forum of Colorado, and as an author. In addition to authoring many articles in the field, Mr. Stradley has written three other practical handbooks for in-service teachers: *Supervising Student Teachers* (Interstate Printers and Publishers, 1968), *A Practical Guide to the Middle School*, and *Administrator's Guide to an Individualized Performance Results Curriculum* (The Center for Applied Research in Education, Inc., 1971, 1974).

Mr. Aspinall has been an educator for 23 years. During that period he has been a classroom teacher, building administrator, and central staff administrator. In his 18 years as administrator, he has been in charge of curriculum programming at the elementary, middle, and high school levels. He has also worked in the International School in Brussels, Belgium, and has given direction to many innovative programs such as departmental team teaching and individualized instruction.

Discipline in the Junior High / Middle School:

A Handbook for Teachers,
Counselors, and Administrators

Richard W. Fraley

About This Book

Teachers and other educators working with middle/junior high students usually feel this age group is the most difficult group with which to work as far as classroom discipline is concerned. Often, children at the "middle age" are labeled unruly, uncooperative, misunderstood, unpredictable, lacking self-discipline, and hardheaded. This age level also reveals traits such as sensitiveness, feelings of insecurity, desire to be recognized, and need for directive understanding and guidance. Middle level teachers are constantly looking for ideas, methods, and techniques that will help them work more effectively with the paradoxical entities known as pre and early adolescents. *Discipline in the Junior High/Middle School* has been written to meet this need. It places special emphasis on the specific areas about which middle school and junior high teachers have expressed most concern—respect for authority, peer relationships, student-teacher conflicts, attendance, group and individual behavior, and vandalism.

This book gives middle level teachers proven methods and techniques for solving the student behavior problems they face when working with early adolescents. The ideas presented were selected on the basis of practicality, adaptability to differing teacher needs, and relationship to the special needs and functioning patterns of early adolescents. They were also selected on the basis of their potential effectiveness in learning situations, as well as for their usefulness as effective discipline techniques.

The practical techniques provided in the book should enable staff members to deal successfully with many pre and early adolescent behavioral problems related to student developmental and maturation conflicts, student-peer and student-teacher differences, student program problems, poor attendance patterns, vandalism, and negative student conduct in the classroom. A variety of possible, workable solutions are provided in each case, so that the teacher can refer to the book for a number of effective techniques and select one method or combination of methods to try in a particular situation.

The book should also be a great time-saver for the teacher, placing at his fingertips specific techniques for dealing with all kinds of everyday problems he faces in working with pre and early adolescents. Following a specific problem/solution format, it covers all areas of discipline—from behavioral problems to stealing and destruction of property, from dress to disrespect, and from classroom to out-of-school activities. Use of this book should enable the teacher to be more effective, allowing him to devote more time and effort to instructional needs and less time to discipline demands.

Discipline in the Junior High/Middle School is designed not only to provide the teacher with practical, proven techniques for disciplinary action, but also to stimulate his thinking in developing more positive solutions to student conduct problems arising in his own classroom. The authors recognize the need for middle level teachers to be concerned about student developmental guidance as well as more direct, blunt corrective action approaches. Therefore, they have included methods and ideas that the teacher can use as the bases for classroom learning activities directly related to improvement of student discipline. These methods and suggestions can be easily incorporated into class activities dealing specifically with early adolescent development, such as Human Relations, Self-Discovery, Individual Guidance, and Self-Direction.

The important factor here is the teacher's use of behavioral development techniques as integral, positive instructional tools. If they are used in this way, students do not tend to view them only as negative methods associated only with misbehavior. This helps to keep learning demands on a positive level and avoids the situation where both the teacher and student attempt to function together at a positive learning level and a negative disciplinary level.

William E. Stradley
Richard D. Aspinall

Contents

6. TECHNIQUES FOR REDUCING ATTENDANCE PROBLEMS (*Continued*)

7. REDUCING ACTS OF VANDALISM   146

8. SOLVING BEHAVIOR PROBLEMS OUTSIDE THE CLASSROOM   160

Discipline in the
Junior High / Middle School:

A Handbook for Teachers,
Counselors, and Administrators

1

Using Preventive Discipline Approaches

Commonly, "discipline" is considered in a negative vein; that is, it is usually related, in practice, to some student violation of an established rule or regulation related to the way the student is expected to conduct himself within a particular interaction framework. Teachers generally function in terms of this negative approach, and students become conditioned to the negative interpretation of "discipline." This in itself leads to interaction conflicts. In taking the positive approach to discipline and the development of self-discipline and self-direction, "discipline" is placed in the same functioning, learning category as the other aspects of the school program, and thereby dovetails with them.

HOW TO USE: STUDENT PLACEMENT
IN PREVENTING DISCIPLINE PROBLEMS

The level of satisfactory student conduct, in most cases, is directly related to how well the functioning demands made of the student are matched with his operational capabilities and the extent to which student, parent, and teacher cooperate in setting the functioning demands. This involvement must be a continuous process, like other learning phases of the program, utilizing the setting of objectives, implementing action processes, and assessing results. This begins from the first day the student enters the school.

Traditionally, student placement is determined by impersonal, arbitrary criteria such as test scores, previous teachers' rating sheets, and anecdotal records referring to unknown functioning frameworks. These have a place, but they should be considered as only a part of the information needed to place a student accurately in or at a learning level. Additional important placement criteria are those identified by the student and parent in relation to:

1. What the school expects of the student.
2. What the student expects of the school.
3. What the parent expects of both the student and the school.
4. What specific student needs/interests have been identified.

These are the human aspects of learning placement and, as a result, they assume a very important role in the student's attitudes toward functioning success. Emphasis of these personalized functioning aspects also helps the student's teachers, counselors, and parents develop more of a commitment to the student's needs, feelings, and limitations. In addition, the cooperative development of a learning framework for the student should be accomplished jointly by parents, teacher, counselor, and student.

As a starting point, a functional way of keeping the human aspects of learning consistently in the minds of the teacher and parent is the utilization of a form such as that shown in Figure 1-1.

The use of such a student assessment chart encourages the teacher to take time to sit down with the student and parent and talk seriously and specifically about the child's individual program of studies, the bases for its development, and the specific reasons why the schedule was developed. The use of such a form by the school staff also encourages the parent, together with his child, to analyze expectations of each other in terms of common objectives related to the student's education.

The utilization of this type of approach on a continuing basis also enables the teacher to have a consistently up-dated record of changes pertaining to the student's and parent's attitudes, expecta-

STUDENT ASSESSMENT CHART

Student _Frank Archer_   Grade _8_

Counselor _Mr. Floyd_   Date _Sept. 7, 19–_

Student Needs	*Interests*	*Expectations of Student*	*Parent*
Making friends	Trumpet	Tryout for	Special reading help
Self-discipline	Basketball	teams	Keep me informed
More men teachers	Shop	Classes that	of his progress
Opportunities to	Getting a job	will help me	Help him gain self-
do work outside the		get a job	confidence
classroom because of		Help me with	Teach him how to
hyperactivity		my reading	study
Reading help			

CLASS SCHEDULE (1st Quarter)   SCHOOL

1. Advanced Band

2. Developmental Reading

3. Shop

4. Basic Electricity (Science/Math)

5. Human Relations

6. General Math

Student and parent keep teachers informed of problems

Parent meets regularly with teachers

Student follows conduct expectations

Student is responsible for own actions

Student meets regularly with teachers to inform them of his assessment of his progress

Copy to each teacher

Figure 1-1

tions, and demands as they relate to the functioning of the school staff. In addition, it allows teachers to make adjustments more quickly and easily in their own planning and consequent operation of demands to parallel the learner changes.

A further advantage derived from this type of form is that it can be used for parent, student, and teacher meetings several times during the year to assess learner progress and to identify together any consequent need changes. Together, then, they can work to develop variations in the student's program of study that will keep his learning emphasis more in line with his needs.

HOW TO USE: TEACHER-STUDENT PLANNING
TO ACHIEVE ACCEPTABLE CONDUCT

Primarily, teachers write lesson plans in terms of the subject matter they teach. In most cases, their identified learning objectives are also limited to student performance in terms of content. Little, if any attention is devoted to planning classroom activities in terms of specific conduct performance needs of the learners.

Class activities are developed around subject content criteria while student conduct is determined by teacher expectations on an acting-reacting basis. Planning, in terms of student actions on the basis of class learning activity demands related to levels of learning difficulties, student performance capabilities, student frustration levels, extents of physical activity, and student self-direction requirements, should be an integral part of the instructional planning process. These need to be identified in terms of specific revealed student functioning characteristics on an ongoing basis.

Planning in a sixth grade math class serves as an example here.

Student Characteristics (heterogeneous group)	Selected Activities	Student Discipline Demands
1. Some students—immaturity (Maturation)	1. Individual counseling by teacher	1. Completion of assigned areas within a prescribed period of time
2. Some students—learning difficulties	2. Individual study at level of learning	2. Understanding and practical use be demonstrated before proceeding to a new area of learning
3. Some students—poor math concept background	3. Additional help through student assistants, parent volunteer tutorial services on a one-to-one basis	3. Concentrate on accuracy and reproduction
4. Some students—strong math concepts basic background	4. Conceptual development through class, group, and individual instruction	
5. Some students—learning extended beyond grade level	5. Development of sufficient practice materials to meet the individual needs	
6. Wide emotional adjustment levels	6. Utilization of challenging materials beyond the confines of the grade level	

The fact that certain learning activities demand particular overt functioning skills must not be overlooked by the teacher. He must incorporate functioning demands, both student and teacher, in the classroom structural design through the setting of performance objectives, selection of specific learning activities, and revealed performance appraisal. All of this planning, selection, implementation, and appraisal is related to teacher functioning as well as student functioning. The two cannot be treated in isolation from each other. In the final analysis, this means planning, implementation, and appraisal are one from the standpoint of the student as the primary functioning emphasis, with the teacher serving in a supportive, facilitating role.

The basic responsibility here is for the teacher to develop adequate processes and skills to identify accurately the location of the student along the learning continuum, the needs and skills of the student, and the operational demands made of the learner. The next step is for the teacher to recognize the role, responsibilities, skills, and modes of operation that will be demanded of him in order to facilitate the attainment of the identified learner/instructor/program objectives. In essence, this means identifying "where the teacher needs to be" in terms of "where the student is."

TEACHER ASSESSMENT CHART

Course _Reading_   Period _2_   Teacher _Conway_

Student Skills	Needs	Teacher Function
1. Reading 1 grade below level	1. Individual help	1. Individualized help
2. Can express thoughts	2. Extra reading at home	2. Consistent appraisal and feedback to student
3. Knows his weaknesses	3. Expand attention span	3. Setting of teacher-student objectives
4. Can follow directions	4. Encouragement/praise	4. Emphasize discussion techniques
		5. Develop a progress time line

Figure 1-2

Teaching effectiveness is determined to a large extent by the teacher's always knowing "where he is" in terms of "where the student is." Staff utilization of a Teacher Assessment Chart such as that shown in Figure 1-2 helps teachers to view student progress continuously in terms of specific student needs and consequent teacher functioning demands. The chart provides a means by which the teacher can more readily develop an ongoing plan of action for both the student and himself.

The use of the Teacher Assessment Chart in connection with the Student Assessment Chart provides the teacher with an adequate functional plan of direction as he develops the classroom learning structure, from both the academic and behavioral standpoints. The information provided by the completed forms, in actuality, is the plan of action for both the student and the teacher.

The Teacher Assessment Chart can also be used by the teacher as a guide for the development of more personalized approaches to discipline with individual students. As the teacher structures his own functioning patterns in terms of identified student needs, he becomes more cognizant of the student's learning and behavioral patterns. As a result, the teacher can more readily dovetail content and conduct demands in terms of specific desired results and operational consistency.

Parent understanding is also facilitated by the use of the chart. When the teacher uses the Student Assessment Chart in parent-student-teacher conferences, he can more easily, by record rather than by memory, discuss specific student needs and his own specific instructional emphases.

HOW TO USE: IDENTIFICATION OF STUDENT FUNCTIONING PATTERNS TO ACHIEVE ACCEPTABLE CONDUCT

Student conduct requirements cannot be separated from the performance patterns of the teacher, the performance demands of the program, or from the everyday performance patterns of the learner. All of these must be dovetailed in a reinforcing way. Identification of the levels of the teacher, the program, and the student must be made, however, before this dovetailing can be done. Generally, attempts are made to do this only in terms of the student, after he reveals a need for some kind of a common denominator of behavior which applies to all students.

Class Demands	Student Responsibility	Teacher Responsibility
1. Setting of performance objectives	1. Identification of learning objectives	1. Identification of learner/teacher objectives
2. Demonstrated ability for student self-direction	2. Self-appraisal of progress	2. Individualization of instruction
3. Develop a sequenced plan of learning	3. Follow a sequenced results time line	3. Develop a sequenced applied performance time line
4. Use of research skills	4. Demonstrate organizing and writing skills	4. Provide for independent study

In an attempt to improve teaching-learning effectiveness, educators are moving toward individualization of instruction in the formal content areas and methods. Since learner conduct is an integral part of the total learning process, it follows that the development of the individualization of student conduct must be a center of teacher focus. This is especially important at middle school level because of the singular developmental changes each student is experiencing.

SPECIAL STUDENT TRANSFER REQUEST

_____West_____ School

Date: _____   _19–_ . _19–_

Student: __R. Brown__ Subject __7th history__

Grade Level: __7__   Time __1:30-2:15 p.m.__

Quarter: __1__   __2__   __3__   __4__

Reason for Transfer Request   _Discipline Referral–talking–unable to sit and concentrate on_

subject matter–bothers other students–extremely nervous

Orientation: Small group or individualized study with tutorial support

Room and/or Area Assignment: _Room 108–Social Studies_

team center–team teacher

Copies to: ___Parent___   ___Counselor___   ___Team___

___Ass't. Prin.___

Figure 1-3

As the teacher works to develop an individualized learning program for each learner, he must take into consideration these maturation changes the student is undergoing and consider them as basic aspects to the development of the teaching-learning structure. Since these pre and early adolescent changes are going to occur at different times and to different extents in the students, it is only common sense for the teacher to accept the changes in each student and vary the functioning demands accordingly. This makes it necessary for the teacher to identify as one of his primary responsibilities the gaining of as much information as possible about each student, his motivational forces, and his day-to-day functioning characteristics. Two aids that are useful in this process of information-gathering are shown in Figures 1-3 and 1-4.

Changes in Student	*Functioning Changes by Teacher*
1. Increased desire for independence	1. Provide opportunities for student to help select his methods of study
2. Increased moodiness	2. Allow for changes of pace and time for student to work by himself or just talk with someone
3. Becoming more agressive	3. Provide some physical activity, also some individual cause/results counseling
4. Increasing concern about his future	4. Include some units on career education; refer also to counselor

When the teacher accepts this basic premise and gains the skills to gain ongoing information about the learner, he is going to find that, more and more, he is thinking primarily in terms of students, rather than subject matter, as he develops his classroom learning structures, methods, and procedures.

As he continues to develop this skill of planning in terms of the student, the teacher will find that he is becoming more proficient in predicting student conduct because he is developing his classroom demands more in terms of the learner functioning capabilities. As the teacher continues to increase his planning and implementation levels in terms of students, he will also find that he is having much more success in developing a positive classroom learning environment because he is using a preventive, rather than a remedial, approach in developing and controlling student conduct characteristics.

```
┌─────────────────────────────────────────────────────────────────────┐
│                 STUDENT SPECIAL SCHEDULING REPORT                      │
│                                                                         │
│                        West    School                                  │
│                                                                         │
│   School Year   19–  –  19–              Semester 1 or 2               │
│                                            (please circle)             │
│                                                                         │
│   Student Name          Special Need            Orientation            │
│     J. Jones              Advanced Math          Individualized study   │
│                                                                         │
│   Level of Capability   Personal Characteristics   Grade Level         │
│     High +                Very conscientious            8               │
│                                                                         │
│   Recommendation:  Programmed Geometry with teacher advisor assigned   │
│                                                                         │
│   Room Assignment:  IMC or Math Resource Center                        │
│                                                                         │
│   Time Schedule:    8:30 a.m. to 9:30 a.m.                             │
│                                                                         │
│   Copies: to: _____ Dept. – _____ Chairman     │
│               _____ Counselor – _____ Records Secretary │
└─────────────────────────────────────────────────────────────────────┘
```

Figure 1-4

HOW TO USE: RECOGNITION OF DIFFERING BEHAVIORAL CAUSES TO IMPROVE BEHAVIOR

The teacher does not have to possess the specialized knowledge of the psychologist in order to recognize the many causes behind student misbehavior. He can identify causes if he takes time, through observation and communication, to become better acquainted with the student and if he continues to develop his instructional/learning demands in terms of the learner's capabilities and characteristics. The teacher does not have to take a clinical approach to behavior problems, but he does need to know how to differentiate between causes and symptoms related to misconduct. Techniques the teacher can use here include the following:

1. Conferences with parent
2. Use of video tape to analyze both teacher and student action patterns

3. Teacher analysis of class demands
4. Selected one-day units on group conduct
5. Study of class group interaction
6. Identification of student weakness in terms of class activities
7. Recognition of student frustration levels
8. Identification of individual student maturation changes

HOW TO HANDLE: SPUR-OF-THE-MOMENT OFFENSES

At the pre and early adolescent level, student misconduct action is often a spur-of-the-moment facetious thing. Since it is a brief action with little thought behind it, quite often a simple, quiet, reprimand from the teacher will be sufficient. Other times, however, the misconduct problem is of a more serious nature. Problems such as continuous student disturbance, maladjustment, consistent frustrations, and insubordination, as examples, should demand more serious teacher attention. They also require decision-making processes of both short- and long-term consideration on the part of the teacher.

Usually, the teacher must determine, here, whether the misconduct demands remedial action. Basically, he must determine this in terms of counseling need or formal disciplinary action. He must make this decision on the basis of the misconduct situation and the performance background of the student. As he makes this decision, he is also determining what support people will be involved, and the roles demanded of these persons.

HOW TO HANDLE: MORE SERIOUS PROBLEMS

If the teacher determines that the misconduct is serious enough to demand immediate and formal action, he usually involves the appropriate school administrator by using a form such as the one shown in Figure 1-5.

This usually means the teacher recognizes a need for discipline that is symptomatic of deeper problems. If he views the situation as more of a counseling need, the appropriate school administrator usually does not need to be formally involved until such time as the counselor and teacher deem necessary or advisable.

DISCIPLINE REFERRAL

STUDENT NAME	TELEPHONE	GRADE	DATE	TIME

REFERRED BY _____

DESCRIBE INCIDENT:

HAS THIS OR SIMILAR BEHAVIOR OCCURRED BEFORE?	INDICATE CORRECTIVE STEPS TAKEN TO DATE:
( ) YES ( ) NO HOW MANY TIMES? _____	( ) WARNINGS AND LECTURES (APPROX. NUM.) _____ ( ) DETENTIONS (APPROX. AMOUNT OF TIME) _____ ( ) PARENT CONTACT ( ) COUNSELOR CONTACT ( ) OTHER _____ ( ) NONE

STUDENT STATEMENT:

ACTION TAKEN: (FOR OFFICE USE)	REMARKS:
( ) CONFERENCE WITH STUDENT ( ) DETENTION _____ HOUR(S) ( ) APOLOGY REQUIRED TO _____ ( ) PARENT PHONE CONTACT ( ) LETTER SENT HOME ( ) COPY OF REFERRAL SENT HOME ( ) PARENT CONFERENCE ( ) REFERRED TO COUNSELOR ( ) SUSPENSION OF _____ DAYS ( ) ISOLATION OF ____ DAYS ( ) OTHER:	

_____
ASSISTANT PRINCIPAL

CC: ( ) REFERRAL TEACHER   ( ) PARENT   ( ) ASSISTANT SUPERINTENDENT   ( ) COUNSELOR   ( ) FILE   ( ) OTHER _____

Figure 1-5

Problem	Referral	Remedial Action
1. Truancy	1. Administration	1. Conference with administrator
2. Rudeness	2. None	2. Conference with student; setting of new behavior objectives/demands
3. Failure to do work	3. Counselor	3. Conference with counselor, parent, and student; analysis of student skills and frustration levels
4. Hyperactive	4. Counselor	4. Study student records for past history; talk with parent; arrange for physical activity
5. Stealing	5. Administrator and Counselor	5. Parent-teacher-counselor-administrator conference; continued observation of student; provide recognition of student in other ways for student ego satisfaction

In the counseling approach, the teacher may want another person to get involved in working with the student or he may prefer an approach that is more subtle and continuing. Hopefully, the student will not view immediate action as disciplinary, but more of a need to work with someone who can help him develop more appropriate patterns of action.

SUPPORT PERSONNEL CATEGORIES

Professional	Nonprofessional
Psychiatrist	Teacher Aides
Psychologist	(can be professional)
Specialist (skill areas)	Parent Volunteer
Team member	Student Assistant
Counselors	Community Resource Person
Librarians	

The decision of the teacher will also determine his own present and follow-up actions. For effectiveness and consistency it is essential that the teacher work in a manner that parallels the approach of whatever support person he asks to become involved. Since there often are decided differences in the approaches taken by the support administrator and the support counselor, it is necessary that the teacher be aware of the action the support person is taking and implement any needed follow-up action on a continuing basis in the classroom. The remedial/preventive action can be ineffective unless the teacher adopts the classroom demands to parallel the action of the support person.

It is important that all appropriate school personnel receive a copy of the discipline referral form. The individual who initiates the form must know that appropriate action has taken place, and also the nature of the action. Support personnel such as parents, counselor, and psychologists must also know the history and recommendations pertaining to such action. The Discipline Referral Form, Figure 1-5, has a special area at the bottom of the form which allows for the initiator to know to whom the referral has gone so that a continuing history can be developed and understood.

HOW TO USE: TEACHER ROLES IN DISCIPLINE PREVENTION

Just as in curriculum design and implementation, the teacher must assume the responsibility for playing an important, ongoing role in behavior development. This means that he must become involved as a designer and initiator of behavioral motivation actions and activities. Teacher emphasis must be concerned with the fact that, in the long run, student behavior is a direct result of instructional actions, program functioning demands, and student frequency of performance success.

With this in mind, every staff member must build into his student/teacher activities learning emphasis related to behavior performance. In order to do this effectively, he needs to do this in terms of performance objectives that clearly set direction and functioning levels related directly to teacher-student interaction as both progress through the program continuum. In effect, this necessitates the identification, within the program/classroom/ learning framework, of the specific roles the teacher will assume in each of the learning activities in which the student is expected to engage. As the student progresses along the learning continuum, the role of the teacher should change; that is, his role should become progressively supportive while, at the same time, the student should become progressively more dominant in terms of self-direction and assumption of responsibility for his own action.

Class Activity	Behavior Emphases	Teacher Role
Group Discussion	Respect for others' opinions	Facilitator of discussion
	Acceptance disagreement	Help set discussion guidelines
	Acceptance of constructive criticism	Recognize the leaders and followers and attempt to vary these student roles
	Assume responsibility to work as a group member	As soon as possible, attempt to withdraw from active participation
		Analyze changes in individual student behavior as discussion progresses
		Help students recognize attainment of specific results
		Hold individual conferences with students who revealed difficulty in participating

As this process unfolds, the instructor must keep in mind the differences, in definition and in practice, between supervision needs and student growth needs as related to present functioning demands, maturation stages, and revealed performance application by the student. It is very easy, unfortunately, for the teacher to insist, through application, to maintain an unchanging role of supervision when he has the students functioning "in his way," where no overt conflicts are materializing.

If the student is to progress satisfactorily through the school program according to specific performance objectives, he must be allowed to demonstrate his proficiency in the areas of self-discipline and self-direction as well as in the academic areas. This means the teacher must progressively relinquish greater degrees of his supervisory control to the student as the student demonstrates his capability of handling more responsibility. This is difficult for many teachers to do and to accept, because it poses a threat to them as a result of their doubts about given students justifying teacher judgment.

Sequencing of activity demands is important here. Examples of this sequencing are:

1. Teacher-led discussion and objective-setting
2. Class assignments and assessment
3. Small group discussions and objective-setting
4. Small group assignments and assessment
5. Individualized assignments and objectives-setting
6. Individualized assignments and assessments
7. Independent study, reporting, and appraisal

This sequence can be stopped and recycled whenever the need arises. Also, individual students can be placed at any point, depending on their revealed functioning capabilities.

HOW TO USE: STAFF TEAMING IN THE DISCIPLINE PROCESS

No staff member should expect, or be expected, to know all characteristics of a given student that affect his functioning patterns. Collectively, however, all of the staff members directly involved with the student can be expected to know a great deal about a given student as a result of his functioning within the generally common demands of the program and the singular demands of each instructor's classroom.

It is only natural, then, for the teacher, as he experiences problems with a student, to consult with other teachers to gain additional information about the learner's functioning characteristics and to find out what other teachers have done, successfully and unsuccessfully, about any problem which the student has had in their classes. This exchange of information, techniques, and ideas can provide each teacher with additional knowledge, skills, and approaches to work more effectively with the student.

One of the best opportunities for the staff to evaluate individual student needs is at staff meetings where the topic of the meeting is devoted entirely to student information and there is parallel staff planning of blocks of time.

Team Planning Evaluation	*Total Staff Evaluation*
(Individual student analysis)	(Individual student and small group analysis)
1. Daily basis	1. Total subject matter function
2. Subject matter	2. Total skill evaluation
3. Skills	3. School peer problems as teacher-student problems

The student's counselor can provide valuable assistance here because he often interacts with the student in less formal, out-of-class situations. The counselor also has the advantage of being able to take the position of a "third party" capable of looking objectively at both the instructional and general learning situations. Of primary importance here is the teacher's willingness to accept the counselor's suggestions if he views any contributing factors to the discipline problem as coming from the teacher.

Teacher teaming in terms of student behavior situations is just as effective as teaming in academic areas. If the team approach is individualized, the follow-up is consistent and the staff members reveal personal concerns about helping the student improve. The student is not the only one who profits from this approach. The teachers profit also, because they are participating in problem-solving activities that are developed in terms of practical situations having a direct bearing on their own effectiveness.

A situation in which the authors were involved with three teachers and a counselor is a case in point.

At the end of the first semester, the seventh-grade math teacher was having increasing conduct problems with a fifteen-year-old girl in his class. He asked for a meeting with the two administrators, the girl's counselor, the math department chairman, and another teacher the girl had who was known to get along very well with the girl.

Prior to the meeting each person involved gathered information concerning his working with the girl. As a result, during the meeting the following facts were quickly brought out.

1. The girl had talked several times to the counselor about her home problems, her older brother's picking on her and her parents' fighting.
2. The teacher who got along well with her often took time to visit with the girl about her personal ambitions to be a hair stylist and sent her to visit two beauty salon owners.
   This teacher also taught home economics, a course in which the girl was interested.
3. The department chairman, a class sponsor, had worked well with the girl on various school committees.
4. The two administrators had worked with the girl in terms of her conduct problems. She was resentful at being forced to go to school and "told everything to do." She had to do much of the housework at home. She dated whenever she wanted.
5. The teacher having trouble with the girl often nagged her about her level of work, made few positive remarks about, or to, the girl, talked to her only about math, knew nothing about the girl's background, functioned as a highly authoritarian teacher.

As the group discussed the problem, they developed the following successful procedures and guidelines for the teacher to use in working with the girl:

1. Show interest in the girl's personal ambitions and on an individualized basis, relate her math to her job interests, where possible.
2. Give the girl some responsibility within the classroom structure as a teacher aid.
3. Allow the girl to help make some decisions related to her class work-performance levels, assignment completion schedule; allow her to work sometimes alone in the math resource room.
4. Treat her more in terms of the relatively mature fifteen-year-old she sees herself to be.
5. Take a positive approach based on what the girl has shown she can do, rather than stressing what she had not done.

6. Take time to visit with her on a social basis outside of the classroom; show interest in her as a human being.
7. Be consistent in expectations and deadlines agreed upon by the student, but recognize that she is easily frustrated by situations over which she has no control.

HOW TO USE: LEARNING ACTIVITIES TO ASSIST IN THE DISCIPLINE PROCESS

Since there is a direct relationship between classroom functioning demands and potential student frustrations, and consequent discipline problems, it is imperative that each staff member devote time to the selection of class learning activities that are geared to the success functioning level of each student. Given learning activities demand singular functioning skills, levels, and prerequisite content knowledge. As a result, class learning activities must be selected with the learner's possession of these tools in mind or else the teacher will be demanding more of the student than he can produce. The changing teacher demand here, then, is an instructional insistence on student failure. Failure, in this sense, can have such a negative effect on the pre and early adolescent that it can affect his attitudes even after he has gone on to the senior high school.

The following example illustrates the problem.

Activity	*Skills Needed*
Research paper (purpose: show ability to organize information)	1. On-level reading ability 2. Ability to use library resources 3. Capable of using time well 4. Does not need constant supervision

Student Functioning Characteristics	*Teacher Adjustment*
1. Low interest in reading 2. Works only by teacher-parent insistence 3. Good conversationalist 4. Participates in class but does not do well on written tests	1. Let student use personal experiences 2. Permit student to make an oral report 3. Permit student to use magazines, T.V., radio, etc. 4. Insist on a detailed student plan of action

It is essential that the teacher ascertain students' capabilities through observation and diagnostic tools as well as through student-teacher conferences before he selects appropriate learning activities. This is especially important when a teacher intends to introduce a learning activity in which the student has never before participated. Failure of the teacher to do so can result in negative student functioning because the learner doesn't know how to proceed or does not possess the necessary learning skills. In a case such as this the teacher is more to blame than the student for any resulting behavior problem because he is forcing the student to function in a situation the student is not adequately prepared to handle.

HOW TO USE: STAFF SKILLS TO MEET SPECIFIC STUDENT NEEDS

Commonly heard in school lounges are comments such as "I would much rather teach the honors classes" or "I feel so sorry for those kids in the remedial reading class." Remarks such as these generally reveal teacher instructional preferences and/or attitudes. They do not, however, necessarily reflect the speaker's skills in working with singular student needs. Actions, not words, must determine teaching assignments.

Effective content teaching and behavior development depend on how effectively teacher functioning skills are matched with specific student needs. Perhaps, at the middle level, from the personalized standpoint, the latter could prove more important because pre and early adolescents often are more inconsistent in their overt behavior than they are in their content studies. *Functioning at the middle level demands of the teacher the maximum in flexibility.*

Example: Teacher A has had experience only at the elementary level (4-6). Teacher A was assigned to a math team program which had responsibility for 6-8 grade level math programs, including algebra.

1. Discipline problems were maximal with older students (grade 8 and algebra).
2. Discipline problems were minimal with younger students (grades 6 and 7).
3. Older students were upset at being treated like elementary students. Students complained about (a) too much talking and counseling on the part of teacher,

(b) teacher inconsistency in governing the class (c) discipline tactics such as standing-in-corner, writing a chapter, being seated in the hallway, and (d) teacher inconsistency and unfairness about grading practices. They also complained that quieter and more respectful students were given higher grades.
4. The teacher was openly fearful of older students.
5. The teacher, after much counseling with other staff members, including teachers, counselors, and administrators, was still unable to function at upper level math program.
The team program reassigned his schedule so that teacher will work with younger students.

As administrators and chairman seek to find, hire, and place appropriately prepared teachers in key assignments, it is extremely important that the teacher hired have the skills, experience, and desire to accept the educational responsibilities paralleling that assignment. There are few teachers who can be all things to all students. The program suffers, sometimes disastrously, when misassignment takes place. If a district is to fulfill its professional obligations to a community, teacher hiring practices and appropriate class and subject matter assignments automatically become one of the most crucial considerations administrators will face. Many factors are at play in this matter: (1) cost, (2) preparation, (3) personality, (4) experience, and last but not least, (5) philosophy and desire.

Since, at the middle/junior high level, emphasis should be on the development of a preventive discipline approach, it is important for the school staff to look at student conduct as a structural concern and as an instructional emphasis. As a result, then, learner behavior must also be considered as a staffing concern. This staffing concern means that the matching of staff functioning skills to specific student academic and social needs must be an integral, continuing function within the school scheduling process and of the continuing student-teacher planning process.

Student needs	Teacher Skills
1. Understanding his physical changes	1. Personalized teaching
	2. Reacting to student provided openings for discussion
	3. Working with student at his own level of experience
	4. Understanding individual student needs.

Student needs	Teacher Skills
2. Developing concern for others	1. Sincere concern for student as a person
	2. Capable of criticizing in a gentle positive manner
	3. Helping the student appraise his own actions
	4. Demonstrate on a daily basis his concern for students as human beings
3. Working in the science laboratory	1. Recognizing students' differing levels of coordination
	2. Recognizing student symptons and class activities that lead to student carelessness
	3. Identifying existing student skills in working with fragile equipment
	4. Capable of adjusting his expectations and demands to student capability levels
	5. Organizing units to coincide with student mastery of equipment use

This matching of staff functioning skills to specific student needs necessitates each individual staff member's identifying his specific areas of strength in terms of recognized student behavioral needs as well as academic needs. Though this is not always possible within the inflexible confines of the traditional master schedule framework, it can be done.

Some approaches a school staff can take are:

1. Assigning teachers as advisors to a given number of students.
2. Offering short courses developed in terms of specific student functioning needs taught by a staff member particularly qualified by temperament and background to work with the identified students.
3. Changing student schedules so that class demands are continually coordinated with student functioning levels.
4. Scheduling staff members according to identified performance objectives as well as by content preparation.

HOW TO USE: IN-SERVICE ACTIVITIES

Effective student conduct procedures and results do not just evolve. The teacher must react immediately in response to misbehavior situations. Pre-planning and adequate preparation in terms of human behavior can make the teacher's reactions much more consistent and effective, especially when these are used with a common-sense approach.

One of the main areas for in-service activity for all staff members is a program specifically designed to help the teacher see himself and his actions as the students view them. This can be difficult for some individuals because they view their job responsibilities only as authoritative dispensers of content instruction and/or they lack the intestinal fortitude to attempt to look at themselves and their actions in a possibly negative, and certainly analytic way. Nevertheless, this must be done if they are to function effectively because they must be able to view themselves from both sides of the desk.

Some basic in-service activities pertaining to the development of needed skills here are:

1. Identifying instructional roles and objectives in terms of specific learner objectives.
2. Having staff members view each others instructional behavior for the specific purpose of identifying actions that are followed by changes, positive and negative, in student conduct.
3. Writing lesson plans from the human standpoint first, then adding the content phase to the plans.
4. Developing individual self-analysis instruments.

Another in-service area that is important is related to student-teacher relationships. An effective approach here is the involvement of staff members in the development of human relations units to be taught without any reliance on formal content material. Primary emphasis should be on the interaction between students and teacher in terms of a specific learning objective. Here, the teacher is forced to rely almost exclusively on his experience, his interaction skills, and his motivational skills. From this, then, direct application can be made in the more formal content courses.

A third in-service focus is to work on the humanizing or personalizing of classroom structure. Staff members, in this area, can gain the necessary skills through participating in in-service activities related to interaction analysis, classroom counseling methods, and the development of a program structure that emphasizes primarily an understanding of the maturation stages and desired behavioral (performance) objectives pertaining to pre and early adolescents. Staff members can identify methods, techniques, and instructional functioning roles that facilitate the attainment of the objectives.

A fourth area of value is one in which staff members participate in the development of self-appraisal instruments that can be used as part of the formal building staff "evaluation" procedures. Important items to be included are those such as achievement of specific objectives, identification of specific individual personal growth activities, contributions to total program effectiveness, and specific observable examples of how the individual has made himself progressively less needed by his students.

The major focus here is that the individual teacher participates in developing the criteria for his own performance appraisal. Consequently, he can concentrate on improving himself in specifically identified areas because he has helped develop an appraisal tool that pertains to his singular talents, skills, and functioning situations, and it has then been written in applied performance terms.

Effective classroom management and consequent effective student performance evolves as a result of careful planning and implementation. Learning does not take place in isolation from the student's developing positive functioning patterns related to self-discipline and self-direction. These do not just come about as a result of the learner's passing through any particular developmental stages. They are a result of the teacher's incorporation of those demands along with opportunities and ways for the student to master the necessary skills, in the overall classroom framework.

In order to do this, each individual staff member needs to plan first in terms of the revealed and desired human characteristics, then add the content demands. He must take the approach that conduct is taught just as in content, but not in isolation from the subject matter. He must plan his own actions in terms paralleling the actions he expects from his students. *Learner discipline comes from teacher conduct.* Consequently, it is important that the teacher plan and implement within his instructional framework behavioral demands that govern both him and the learner. As he does this, however, he must be sure that he possesses the necessary skills himself before he demands them from the student.

As a final in-service plan, the professional staff can include in the yearly pre-school orientation program a special meeting concerned only with student behavior and what the school district's goals are relative to both the classroom and total program demands. This meeting provides an opportunity to redefine the teacher's role as it relates to other teachers as well as other parts of the program. The program might include speakers and discussions pertaining to district and building policies. From the standpoint of visual materials, a district might wish to consider using the following materials:

SCHOOL IN-SERVICE PROGRAM FOR
UNDERSTANDING CLASSROOM BEHAVIOR

- *Controlling Classroom Misbehavior* – sound filmstrip
- *Motivation in Teaching and Learning* – sound filmstrip
- *Conferencing as a Way of Solving Discipline Problems* – sound filmstrip

The preceding materials have been developed by the National Education Association.

1. Gnagey, William J., *Controlling Classroom Misbehavior* ($8.00), Order from:
     National Education Association
     Publication-Sales Section
     1201 Sixteenth Street, N.W.
     Washington, D.C. 20036
2. Hamacheck, Don E., *Motivation in Teaching and Learning* ($8.00), Order from:
     National Education Association
     Publication-Sales Section
     1201 Sixteenth Street, N.W.
     Washington, D.C. 20036
3. Anonymous, *Conference Time for Parents and Teachers* ($12.00), Order from:
     National Education Association
     P.O. Box #327
     Hyattsville, Md. 20781

2

Helping Students Improve Their Self-Images

HOW TO USE: DRESS CODES TO AFFECT STUDENT CONDUCT FAVORABLY

There has been considerable discussion as to whether or not dress codes have any effect upon school behavior and attitudes. After collecting the thoughts of many teachers, administrators, and support personnel, we conclude that a great majority of school-related people believe that there is definitely a high relationship between dress codes and conduct in general. Some have gone so far as to conduct minor research projects by having students themselves evaluate conduct under different dress code settings. All aspects of the daily program were compared, and even when students were the only observers doing the comparisons, dress definitely had a bearing on how students acted and responded. As one student said, "When I come grubby, I feel grubby; but, when I come in my school clothes, I know I must work!" The use of the word "school clothes" implies dress code and the dress code automatically implies a seriousness of purpose.

One of the teachers who responded to the question about dress code made this comparison: "I've worked in all kinds of schools and I am firmly convinced that the school which has a dress code, *and enforces the dress code,* comes closer to achieving the true purposes of education which relate to learning and attitude."

The authors' school periodically allows "grub days." However, even when such student council-sponsored days occur, there is still a limit placed upon degree, and propriety and good taste are still

41

the order of the day. There are also offshoots of "grub day" which give vent to certain whims, such as "hat day," "famous character day," and "masquerade day." All of the events, when controlled, can be fun for everyone concerned. It is interesting to note how many middle students will involve themselves in such antics. Teachers have also become involved and a certain amount of competition takes place. The student council usually gives awards for some special type of dress based upon previously prescribed criteria. The idea of temporary change or relaxation helps to instill a degree of student morale which cannot be gained in any other manner.

A typical middle school dress code might be like the one that follows:

The purpose of a dress code is not to inhibit any person's taste in attire, but rather to better facilitate the process of education through reasonable guidelines of "dress." *Modesty and cleanliness are our goals.* Due to the fact that some types of clothing do not encourage students to be aware of the goals as such, the following limitations for boys' and girls' attire are in effect:

Boys' clothing—Boys may not wear ski boots, cut-offs, shorts, or tank-top muscle shirts. Hair must be groomed and clean. Shoes and socks must be worn.

Girls' clothing—Girls may not wear clothing that is too tight, too bare, or so extreme as to be immodest. See-through blouses, halter tops, tank tops, bare midriffs, and some mini-garments fall in this category. If a girl wishes to wear a shorts type of garment, the school will allow the culotte (separated skirt) type of short skirt. Shoes and/or sandals must be worn. Rubber beach shoes or wooden clogs (without rubber sole) are not allowed.

The code is simple and yet has built into it the standards which the community wants for their young.

Many public schools, because of the trends the Supreme Court has taken relative to individual liberty, now have no standards for dress or modesty whatsoever. It seems that the game we are playing might be called: "It is better for all of us to stand for nothing than to have something of dignity to which someone might object."

It is very important when a school is considering the establishment of a dress code that students and parents have input into its formulation. Many school officials have neglected this basic responsibility of involvement.

Various school systems have recommended the following techniques for incorporating a new dress code or changing the present dress code:

1. A student council committee appointed to consider the students' thoughts about a dress code.
2. A PTA special committee to consider community thoughts about a dress code.
3. A faculty-administrative committee to consider building standards for dress.
4. A combined committee to consider the findings of the group committees.
5. A first printing of a proposed dress code with an appropriate place for comments. This might be in the form of a handout or be included in a parent newsletter and the school newspaper.
6. An open meeting of the PTA to discuss the code.
7. Class meetings held by the student council to discuss the code.
8. As community-school thoughts are finalized, incorporation of the dress code.
9. Use of a vote system to incorporate a new set of dress standards. (This is used by a few schools. The authors' experience has shown that educators must make the final decision after giving careful consideration to the thoughts of students and community.)

Dress codes must be updated on a regular basis. It is interesting to note how the names of various types of clothing change with time. New trends should be noted and given consideration. However, the basic dress code should still be established on the basis of good grooming, modesty, and cleanliness.

There are some clothing fads which educators should be aware of because they create a real problem for building personnel. One such fad is that of soft-soled and soft-heeled boots. The cleaning costs for tiled school buildings have skyrocketed because of the marking problems these boots have created. Some students, almost out of maliciousness, have tried to see how much of a problem they could create with such boots. Floors, walls, lockers (kicking and denting) have all been fair game. As a result many schools have said *no* soft-heeled boots.

HOW TO DEAL WITH: PERSONAL CLEANLINESS

One of the most important parts of a dress code is the part which stresses cleanliness. It would seem that with just a little parent supervision this should never be a problem. However, public schools have found it to be a never-ending problem. Many working parents leave the home early and are not around to see that their young people are ready for school. Many parents never get up in the morning to help their young people prepare for school. Recent trends should show parents that young people, as never before, need the love and attention that goes with helping them learn to develop and accept those habits which make for being a happy successful adult. Healthful living parallels cleanliness. Abuse of physical cleanliness can leave just as many psychological scars as can a disease. Both student and parent handbooks should discuss the need for cleanliness, even beyond the dress code. They should also briefly discuss the routines that will be followed when a student has a problem with cleanliness. An example of such a routine might be:

1. The student will be taken to a counselor, who will briefly discuss the problem;
2. If a nurse is available, she will be asked to help show the student the need for cleanliness;
3. If the student tries to solve the problem on his or her own, parents will not be contacted;
4. If the problem persists, parents will be asked for help.

Peers are probably the best source of getting help for a student. In fact, initially, fellow students will usually let the faculty know that a problem exists, and they might even try to solve the problem in a very direct manner. Sometimes students may be so direct and abusive in their approach that they do considerable psychological harm to a fellow student. If such a problem is brought to a teacher's attention by a student, we would recommend that: (a) if the student is a close friend, he be asked to try to broach the subject with the student; (b) the friend and other friends might talk with the student; and (c) the teacher plus the student's friends try to counsel him about his problem. Counselors, nurses and/or doctors, and then parents might be asked to help. Whatever direction is taken, it must be remembered that is a problem which must be dealt with in a professional, tactful manner if it is going to be solved in a positive way.

HOW TO USE: TEACHER COUNSELING TO FOSTER ADJUSTMENT TO DEVELOPMENTAL CHANGES

The middle level school is unique in that it is the time in each child's life when he begins to mature in a physical way. Few days go by during which teachers at this level are not talking about the changes they see and the manner in which students are handling these changes. Working with pre-teens and early teen-agers is one of the beautiful aspects of being a middle level teacher. The counseling done by teachers that parallels this growth period for students is one of the most important facets of middle level education. All members of the faculty find themselves involved with the growing pains of these young people. Much of what teachers find is both humorous and serious. A few of the physical pitfalls that young people must hurdle are reflected in comments like these: (a) "Everybody is staring at me;" (b) "I can't help it that my clothes are too tight, they must have shrunk;" (c) "The buttons on my shirt keep coming unbuttoned;" (d) "Did you notice I cut myself shaving;" (e) "My shirttail just keeps coming out, it won't stay in;" (f) "He embarrassed me in the way he said 'Wow;' " (g) "I won't take that kind of talk from anyone!" All of these statements imply embarrassment about physical maturation. The majority of the statements are meaningless; but, it is how a person interprets them that gives them substance.

Maybe young people want peers and adults to notice their growth. They will do everything in their power to let the world know that they have achieved puberty and a certain degree of sexuality. It is this group that must be counseled regarding extremes and where they can lead. Usually this type of child is very insecure about his growth patterns because he lacks knowledge about what is happening to him inside and out. He does not know how to handle his feelings, and to use a teen term in relation to his involvement with peers, "He blew it." This is why the teachers at the middle level must be carefully selected for their positions. They must be secure adults in their own right, and have enough knowledge about adolescent psychology to apply it from the first day of school. Not everyone can handle a teaching position at this level. It takes considerable talent and effort to cope with the 10-to-14-year age group.

Many students, as puberty occurs, face a very serious traumatic effect. A few never get over it. Parents and elementary teachers as well as the middle school staff must do a lot of pre-counseling so that a child knows what to expect and will not be abused by it. He or she must realize that emotions are tied closely with physical change, which is usually not well understood. The authors have noted that the child whose parents have been open, honest, gentle, and loving is usually the one who comes through this age with the fewest scars.

Every elementary school and lower middle school program should include an "in-service" program for parents concerning the preadolescent, adolescent, and young adult growth patterns. This course should include such topics as: (a) shyness, (b) embarrassment, (c) the need to be alone, (d) the extrovert and introvert, (e) paint and powder, (f) the extremist, (g) the need for the feeling of success some time during each day, (h) sex education, (i) the ability to love and be loved (not in a sexual sense), (j) the ability to care and have feelings about people, animals, and so on.

HOW TO USE: TEACHER COUNSELING TO AVOID
EXCESSIVE DISPLAYS OF AFFECTION

As a child becomes a young adult, his or her interest in the opposite sex becomes apparent. Many articles talk about when a girl begins to watch her figure, and when a boy begins to be meticulous about his hair being combed, his teeth being brushed, and when he shows an interest in bathing and using appropriate lotions. It is at this time in young people's lives that they assume the burdens of the world. They become very serious, moody, and very interested in members of the opposite sex. Again, there is much need to help young people through this stage, for without considerable counseling, tragic mistakes can occur.

Some parents think that it is old hat to talk about dating, respect for one's partner, setting time limits on when to be in, where not to go, and what not to do. Yet, they must realize that it is through such discussions that many young people find a sense of security which is derived from a sense of love and care on the part of parents. Without such help, young people grope for answers.

There are also many parents who feel that young people nowadays already know all of the answers about such things. As educators, we call this the world of bluff. It is true that many grow up too quickly, that many are encouraged and pushed to grow up too quickly, but the majority are no different today than we were at the same age. Yes, language is more open and abusive, but it is not language that dictates the depth of our understandings. A fourteen, fifteen, or sixteen-year-old is still only so old with just so much experience. Maturity comes much later for the majority.

Many students also have a need to show affection toward teachers. This can, in a sense, be embarrassing to a teacher. Yet, with gentleness, a teacher can talk in a fatherly manner about such affection so those students will refrain from the need for physical contact and just walk alongside knowing that the teacher cares and understands.

Teachers use many tactics to combat excessive displays of affection. Most follow patterns such as:

1. Counseling the student about her needs for affection and what is acceptable and not acceptable behavior;
2. If there is a group of children who follow the same pattern, developing a group counseling session which will be able to deal with feelings and needs without reservations;
3. Discussing privately with parents a child's need for affection so that much of his need can be solved within the family.

Teachers should be aware of what children are trying to tell us by their actions. Affection can be transferred from a physical to neutral form just by showing a sincere interest in a person. This will usually suffice for this age group.

HOW TO HANDLE: ROWDINESS AND HORSEPLAY

Quite a few middle level students have a difficult time separating work from play. It is the age of vitality which must be channeled into positive directions. The experienced teacher will readily identify the excess energy long before it becomes a negative problem and will try to redirect it to the class's benefit. There are a few students who border on being hyperactive, who can be controlled with proper medication. However, the child who is always playing around, who enjoys the status of being a rowdy and can never get down to being serious needs special help such as: (a) well-defined and understood rules, (b) specific disciplinary procedures, (c) consistent follow-through with discipline whenever he disrupts the class, (d) special counseling about behavior and behavior patterns, in terms of success and failure, (e) an ultimate disciplinary act if he doesn't settle down, such as removal, spanking, and so on.

The saying "There is a joker in every crowd" is too often true at the middle school level. Need for attention, to be daring, to be physical, to enjoy playing tricks on others are typical traits of students requiring help to overcome the need for overt action so as to be the center of attention.

One teacher indicated that she solved such problems by in fact making the clown a real clown whose sole purpose for awhile was to entertain. Another teacher used up the excess energy of such students by assigning cleanup details on a detention basis. Most teachers, rather than to embarrass or restrict the student, try to redirect the child's energies by using psychology as a means for controlling behavior. One teacher who was driven to a point of exasperation found success when she informed the class that Johnny was rather special because Johnny has never learned how to control himself in a physical sense. Her pat comment for awhile about Johnny and his actions was "You will have to excuse Johnny. He doesn't know any better. He has as yet to learn about not doing things like that." The peer pressure resulting from this approach kept Johnny in line as students began to ostracize him for his inability to learn and conform to a degree.

A teacher in a large city middle school said he used many approaches which followed a specific pattern. The following illustrates his techniques: (a) a look of being perturbed, (b) a mean glance, (c) walking over to the side of the student and having a few words about his conduct, (d) an embarrassment by standing the student in the corner with his back to the class or sitting him right alongside the teacher with his back to the class, (e) physically taking him to the vice principal, (g) removal from class for a specific period of time and having a parent conference. The teacher indicated that if a pattern of behavior was developing, the earlier the parent conference the better.

HOW TO HANDLE: DRAWING ATTENTION TO ONESELF

The majority of items in this chapter involve a student's attempt to draw attention to himself. The questions to be asked are "Why is he doing this, and what are his needs?" Trying to find the answers to such questions is not an easy task and takes time. One of the best places to start looking for solutions is at a meeting where all of his teachers are assembled. The sharing process about such a problem is an interesting one. If the student is new to the school system, that would be the time to go over his past records in a thorough manner. The input of each teacher as to how the child acts in his class is important. Some teachers who are not having troubles should compare the ways that they treat the child, and so on. Those who are having troubles should also compare the child's conduct in their classes and what techniques each has used in trying to bring the child to a point of acceptable behavior. The parents should then be notified that school personnel are having some difficulty and are sharing information as to how to solve the problem. It is important that the contract with parents be made, for it tells them that the teachers are willing to try to solve the child's problems. The parents should be asked at this time for any additional information which they possess which should be shared with the faculty. If so, the parents should be asked to come to the school for a conference with all of the child's teachers, counselor, and possibly administrators. At the time of this conference the child might be asked to accompany the parents. This is recommended but is not always necessary.

It is interesting to note what happens to a child's image of himself when involved in such a procedure. He cannot admit that there is a problem, and usually if parents are supportive of the schools efforts, the child realizes that he must make some changes. If the conference continues on a positive basis, the child will know that all are seeking answers to his dilemma and he will be positive in return. The questions asked of him can be very leading and should provide some insight into how he views his actions and his problems. Teachers just might find out how frightened he is at being in a new school, how he thinks his peers and teachers view him, what he thinks of the school per se, how he views the program, in terms of how it has been developed to meet his needs, and what he thinks of the various teachers and especially their treatment of him as a student. The answers to all of these questions will be quite enlightening, especially as they relate to what information the parents have to share with the faculty.

There will be times when, even with all of this sharing of information, nothing seems to work. If the student continues to seriously upset the class routine, the parents and school personnel might have to reach for special medical and psychiatric help. Special schools have been developed to serve special student needs and being assigned to such a school might be the best answer. School authorities should not feel that for every student so placed they have failed. Many such schools are the answer to specific student needs. One always hopes that it is not long before the student can return to the regular classroom.

Even though many students do not understand the reasons for this action, they do in their way tell us that they have concerns and need help to solve these problems. If we are wise enough to listen, we might save them years of frustration and failure.

HOW TO HANDLE: RUDENESS AND POOR MANNERS

This could be a two-sided problem. Why is a child rude and why are his manners so poor? Many times the training that a student has received from home falls quite short of school expectations. How does a teacher find out if this is the case or if in fact the student is using such behavior as an attention-getter? It behooves the teacher to start very gently in trying to solve the problem, for if in fact it is a training problem, considerable work and counseling will have to take place with the student, parents, and family. This can be a ticklish problem because of differing mores. However, if the student is to stay in the school system, he will have to know what is to be expected of him, and hopefully, parents will support the school's position.

If the child is acting out his problems in order to get attention, and in fact behaves differently at school than at home or elsewhere in the community, he is trying to tell someone that he has a problem and that he does not know how to solve it. If not handled correctly, this kind of child winds up as a pure discipline case even though his problem should have been handled in a more gentle manner. So that this does not happen, a teacher should make her concern known about the child's behavior, and again receive input from other staff members about his overall behavior.

The child who is rude is usually rude most of the time. Sullenness and rudeness often go together. They are signs of deep-seated personality problems which are difficult to solve. If these traits persist, school officials should ask parents to seek professional psychiatric help for their child. If the traits are displayed just at school, school personnel should look closely at various techniques to help the child work through his animosities or fears. A few such techniques are:

1. Identifying his favorite classes and the reasons why they are his favorites;
2. Pinpointing the areas in which he is experiencing success and
3. Determining whether he has a learning disability and, if so, how long he has had trouble in special areas of the curriculum;
4. Determining whether he needs to receive considerable encouragement and statements of praise in order to feel success.

When several of these techniques have been followed through, teachers should observe any behavioral change that may result. Does the child try not to display poor manners? Does his rudeness stop? It should be remembered that the solving of such problems does not usually occur overnight; they must be dealt with patiently but with persistence on the faculty's part.

HOW TO HANDLE: STUDENTS WITH PROBLEMS
OF PHYSICAL DEVIATION

Many students find themselves having to cope with physical problems which seemingly make them different from other young-sters. It makes little difference to the child who has such problems whether he is obese, skinny, too short, too tall, or has something congenitally wrong. The fact is that he is different and he knows it. Of all the different children which teachers work with, many of these types are the most heart rendering. How does one tell an obese child to forget his problem and go ahead and live a normal life? How does one tell the child with no arms that he must face his problem head on, accept the challenge and, hopefully, with the miracles of modern-day inventions he can lead a more normal life? Such types of physical afflictions usually have a tendency to scar one's personality, and the problem which all teachers must face in working with such children is how to keep the scar from being permanent. There are many suggestions for working with young people who are so handicapped. A few are: (a) be understanding but do not pity, (b) be encouraging and helpful when needed but do not overdo so as to single out the student, (c) try to treat the student as you do the other students, (d) if the student needs someone to talk to, be a good listener, and if asked for suggestions give them, (e) and never condescend to do the work for such a student, for this is interpreted as pity and can in fact become a trait that the student will expect from others.

The parents and family of such children will probably need help in coping with the child's behavior patterns and his problems. Quite often various members of the family of a child with such problems will also be different in the same respect. If this is the case, the counseling, help, and understanding needed will probably be easily achieved. It the child is unique in his difference, family counseling will undoubtedly be needed on a rather long-range basis.

The question is often asked, "Should we treat such children in a special way, special privileges, etc.?" There is no single answer, nor is there a single solution. As you work with the child let common sense be your guide. The authors have found that such young people need a special kind of understanding, and sometimes special treatment. Whereas the understanding must be continuous, the special treatment will depend upon the circumstances. Students having these problems will usually, in their way, let you know if they need special help.

Handicapped children will need preferential treatment regarding special parts of the curriculum. Do not be hesitant to grant such treatment.

Example: An extremely obese child does not want to take physical education. The first thing that comes to the mind of the teacher of such a class is that of all the things this child needs, he needs physical exercise. However, even though a medical doctor might agree with the teacher, the child also has other fears that must be overcome simultaneously. He does not want to undress in the presence of other students. A recommended procedure in this case is to (a) allow him privacy even though you might have to use a custodial closet; (b) if there is a shower requirement, either make sure that he can take such privately, or excuse him from the requirement; (c) grade him upon his willingness to get involved, not upon his physical performance; (d) if dressing out is the problem (i.e., shorts, t-shirt), allow him to wear something like a sweat suit if it helps him solve the problem of being with the group. If it is physically impossible for the child to participate, do not hesitate to assign him to a quiet area where he can study. One student with an obesity problem enjoyed walking for exercise, and recommended that he be allowed to walk around the stadium track during the physical education class. He kept track of the number of times that he could do this, and was even able to go from 21 to 32 times in a 50-minute period. Later on, another student with a similar problem joined him. Whereas these students had originally been very negative toward the school and especially the P.E. class, they eventually became very positive toward the school since they felt that their needs were being met. As a result of this positive experience, the hot lunch program joined in helping meet dietary needs by fixing for these students a special lunch which was aimed at helping them lose weight.

There is one other technique that should be kept in mind when working with such children. It could be called the "balance system." Using a counseling system, different children must be shown that in some respect we are all different. Many of our differences cannot be seen in a physical way, and as a result they go unnoticed. However, if the truth were known, most people must make allowances for certain weaknesses and capitalize on special strengths. Just because some weaknesses are not physically evident does not mean that they are not, in a sense, a chain round a person's neck. School personnel must look for and make sure that such children understand what attributes they possess. These attributes then become the points of success which can help see a child through each day. A few such attributes to look for are: (a) humor, (b) intelligence, (c) ability to write, spell, do math, (d) ability to write or recite poetry, (e) strength, (f) gentleness, (g) ability to work with younger children, (h) hobbies, (i) complexion, (j) eyes, (k) hair, (l) dress. Compliments are free and they can change a person's life if given honestly. All it takes is a little interest in the individual.

HOW TO HANDLE: BULLYING

Every school has its bullies. The majority of such students do not become bullies overnight. Much of what they emulate is a direct result of problems which directly stem from their home life. There are many factors which play on children to lead them in this direction. A few such factors are: (a) the way they are treated by parents (if abused they will tend to abuse), (b) size (whether large or small they seem to always have to prove themselves), and (c) a feeling of insecurity.

When a teacher notices a student who is slowly developing those characteristics which lead to bullying, he should immediately bring this fact to the student's attention. Many students do not understand that the trait of bullying is a learned one taking many years to develop. The teacher should also inform the student that he will not tolerate this kind of behavior, because of the intimidation factor toward other students. Such a student will usually challenge a teacher and the teacher had better be prepared with a plan of action. If the initial confrontation is handled properly and the student discontinues the bullying pattern, the teacher should make a note to the effect of what has happened and what the results are so that if it occurs again he will immediately take rather strenuous measures to end such a trait once and for all. Teachers should share the information that such and such a student is moving in this direction and that they should all be consistent in their handling of his child's problem.

If the student decides to challenge the teacher about his right to bully and intimidate, the teacher will probably have to reach for the help of the building administrator in charge of discipline. Parents can be very helpful in solving this problem, if they are thoroughly apprised of their child's actions.

School personnel must be specific as to what type of disciplinary measures are going to be taken if the student persists in committing bullying acts. Suspension is usually an initial step, followed by limiting the student's school time. When this occurs, parents must personally bring their child to school and pick him up. If anything happens during this time block, the student might then be placed on a home-bound basis with tutorial services being sent to the home. Once a student is so restricted, if he continues in his harrassment of students, the police are then involved.

It is an interesting fact that if bullies are not stopped early in the developing stages of such behavior, they quickly move in the direction of becoming practiced extortionists, thieves, and so on. Therefore, it is imperative that school personnel do everything in their power to change the direction such a child is traveling.

Bullies also tend to develop gangs, for in group action there is more strength. A gang movement within a school can create real fear. That is why teachers should be looking for students who are moving in this direction from the first day of school, and try to redirect their energies with positive channels such as athletics, hobbies, student council, and drama or music productions.

HOW TO HANDLE: SHOWING OFF FOR VISITORS

Why is it that some students will behave in a perfectly normal way until that time when visitors are present? All teachers, when they know that visitors are coming, should talk with their class about how to behave when the visitors are present. They should also explain why the visitors are coming to the school. It is not that the teachers will know who might act up, but there are students who have such tendencies, and their counsel is usually for them. This pre-counseling technique is the best way to head off such problems. It takes a few minutes of class time but it is time usually well spent. The teacher should note when she did such, and maybe she should even tape her comments so that the class knows that a record of them is being kept. Then, if a child does create a problem and parents are called in, a replaying of the tape is all that is needed for beginning a disciplinary action. One teacher used this technique but forgot to take role to see who was absent. It turned out that the only student who gave problems was the one who was absent that day. From that day on she has used this technique along with an attendance check. Any student who was absent was required to listen to the tape prior to the time that visitors were to arrive.

A teacher should always be able to leave a class unattended, have visitors, or incorporate some change without worrying about student behavior. In one school, one of the authors, for a time, served as a teacher-superintendent. Since there was considerable overlap of responsibilities, he spent considerable time preparing the students for those moments when he might not be present. The routine developed began with attendance, then lesson plans, and finally, assignments. Volunteers were solicited to help. On days when the teacher-superintendent would arrive late to a class he would sit in the back of the classroom and allow the volunteers to continue the teaching experience. Gradually the class began to accept the leadership of those students who were excelling in that subject. The classes were proud of their accomplishments and to this day members of these classes still talk about a beautiful, unique experience in which they played a major role.

HOW TO HANDLE: EXCESSIVE DEFENSIVENESS

Middle level students who find themselves not quite ready to accept all of the responsibilities that go with their age group often become very defensive about their involvement in the growing up process. No one can seemingly involve himself with such a student without receiving some kind of negative retort.

Defensiveness as a trait is often associated with failure, such as one's inability to change a situation that currently exists. As an overreaction it can also imply great concern, such as a student being defensive about his parents, his dad's job, a drinking problem within the home, not having proper clothes, not being able to afford buying a certain item which is needed, or, on the other hand, too much family success and maybe not enough love and respect.

It takes a considerable amount of digging and prying to find out why a student has become so defensive. Oftentimes the problem cannot be brought to the surface, but the student becomes aware of the need to change negative attitudinal traits. Teachers should be very gentle and positive in trying to change such behavior, and sometimes the fact that one first shows an interest is enough to solve the problem. It should be noted that in some classes the student will continue to be very defensive while in others he will show signs of being positive and helpful. The teacher who shows a personal interest will usually be the one to receive positive responses.

HOW TO HANDLE: MOODINESS

One of the most common traits observed at the middle school level is moodiness. It is not usually a long-lasting problem but it is one that creates a certain amount of difficulty for the classroom process. There are many causes for moodiness, but most are the result of the growing-up process. The majority of students can be talked out of a stage of moodiness by the teacher by using a degree of humor or just plain kidding. Others will be offended by such actions, and they have to be left alone to work through the problem creating the mood.

Moodiness can take many forms and mean many things. Worry seems to be the main cause for moodiness in middle level students. It can be associated with grades, friendships, dates, sports, and so forth. As young people try to work through their problems they can easily go from moodiness, sullenness, and defensiveness to complete happiness in just a matter of seconds. So is the world of the middle level student. It might take nothing more than a positive word or a supportive glance to change a student's mood. On the other hand, a teacher can easily precipitate a situation and cause general negative moodiness in a whole class. A couple of examples of how moodiness can be generated: (a) having the whole class retake an exam because a few students cheated, (b) berating a class for some type of group conduct, (c) praising a class for the manner in which they handled a problem such as a fire drill, (d) praising a portion of a class for work accomplished on a research project, and chiding the rest for not being responsible.

A teacher, by the use of psychology, can pretty well control the problem of moodiness. He must be willing, however, to become involved on both an individual and group level if he is going to work with middle level students. His involvement will dictate his success as a teacher at this level.

HOW TO HANDLE: LACK OF PERSONAL PRIDE

The majority of students do not have a problem with pride at the middle school level. Most continue to try to do their best based upon their varying interests and talents. If there is a singular reason for teachers enjoying their work as they teach fifth through ninth graders, it is the uncontrolled enthusiasm and pride which students possess. This is also why the author feels that teachers who teach at the middle level must be extremely dedicated and interested in the profession, for students at this level will drive the less than able teacher out of the profession in a very short period of time.

Students who seemingly have little or no pride in their work or themselves are the negative products of conflicts within a home and society. Whether the home and society have failed them, or they have failed the home and society, is a good question. The fact is that they have few values upon which to build a successful life. It takes a long time and much success to develop an understanding of pride. Middle level teachers have many opportunities to help students understand why personal pride and acceptance are so important. The basic program at most middle level schools and junior high schools is one based upon an experience curriculum. The philosophy does not dictate perfection but implies a considerable sampling of many experiences. Teachers usually try to grade the student upon his own accomplishment and interest and not upon a standardized performance scale. Many call this individualized instruction.

For the few students who have a problem with personal pride, whether it be in dress, writing habits, doing homework, getting to class on time, practicing for band, or personal grooming, the fact is that someone must show them what all of this can mean to them on a long-range basis. Teachers must secure the help of parents relative to standards of job performance. There should be rewards for doing a job well, and time for reflection when the opposite occurs. This should start when a child can demonstrate that he is responsible enough to do some chore. A reward, whatever it may be, is important. Sometimes the reward need be nothing more than a word of thanks. However, most children respond more positively when it is something like candy or money. Teachers might wish to use such items when dealing with such students. If parents and teachers work back to back using the same technique, so much the better.

Praise is one of the most important elements in establishing a sense of personal pride. It should not be overdone but if honestly given, one should not worry about the number of such incidents.

Standards should be set and held to for such students, for it is through standards that they will develop a sense of success. If a student does not do the work, show him that you are disappointed but do not overreact. Encourage him to do better the next time, and when possible use praise.

One new teacher was faced with this type of problem from the very first time the class met. The student was almost defiant toward doing any kind of work. At first she was irritated and then she began to notice that he enjoyed the attention that resulted from her irritation. After talking with parents, she found that if she showed interest but little emotion he did not know how to react to her. She continued to show an interest in him and his work, and finally, after four weeks, he handed in his first paper. It was not much but was the first piece of completed work handed in in a two-year period of time. The teacher shared her knowledge with other teachers and before the year was out, the student was doing average-plus work.

3

Methods for Developing Respect for Authority

It is difficult at times for the middle level teacher to be certain of the pre or early adolescent's motive for any given action. The child himself often is not able to define this clearly in his own mind. The behavioral level of the middle level student varies from obvious insecurity and crying to overt defiance from action to action when he is called to task for his behavior. He experiences conflict between adult demands for respect for, and obedience to, teacher authority and his own felt needs for personal decision-making and respect.

This is often a primary reason for the middle level student's exhibiting a seeming resentment of teacher authority. In addition, the pre or early adolescent is beginning to feel that he is entitled to some of the freedoms traditionally reserved for adults, yet given to older adolescents. Because of this, it is important that the teacher, as he adopts procedures for developing student respect for authority, keep in mind that the corrective measures he takes must be related to student development levels as well as to immediate acts of misbehavior.

HOW TO: ESTABLISH RULES
FOR THE CARE OF MATERIALS AND EQUIPMENT

Middle level students are often simply careless about the manner in which they care for school materials and equipment. In some situations, especially with equipment, students can be deliberately destructive. Students should be made aware of how the teacher will react once he has determined an act to be a result of student carelessness or a desire to destroy or damage.

If materials or equipment have been damaged because of a student's carelessness or neglect, in addition to having the student pay the cost of replacement or repair, the instructor can take the following actions:

1. Have the student sign for each instructional item he needs to use, giving date, time, place, and condition of item. When the item is returned, the teacher and student should note and record the time the item was returned and its condition.
2. If the carelessness still exists, the teacher can require that the student use the item only close to his desk. If the item is to be taken out for use at home, the teacher can request the parent sign for the items and be responsible for their return in good condition.
3. The teacher can let the student use materials that are already in poor condition. When the student learns to care for these, he can be permitted to use those materials in much better condition. This technique works especially well with textbooks and supplementary paperback books.

Several junior high schools in a metropolitan school district found these methods effective for most students. For the smaller number of students who revealed consistent lack of personal concern for school property, two school staff members took these additional actions:

1. Against one student who insisted on destroying materials, taking lenses and other parts from projectors, and taking microphones from recorders, the school filed formal charges to have the student removed permanently from school.
2. In two instances, one school administration initiated referrals to the school psychologist. These students simply had strong desires to take equipment apart to frustrate the teacher. Though finding the reason for the students' actions involved a referral, the solution was relatively simple. The boys were directed not to handle any equipment. If it were proved that they had hidden parts again, they would be recommended for

exclusion from school. For these two boys, this approach worked because their friends were in school. Without friends, there was little to do by themselves.

HOW TO HANDLE: OBSCENE LITERATURE

It is probably safe to say that every school staff must expect to deal with problems related to pornographic material, not only material that is published commercially, but also original works produced by individual students. Interest in this type of material is not something for which most students should be morally condemned. This student interest, however, must be directed into more healthy channels. Teachers, in dealing with obscene literature problems, must be careful not to let their own moral values be the only bases for remedial actions against students. Decisions should be made on the basis of what is best for the student involved.

The following progressive steps can be taken in an effort to help students deal with their growing interests in the opposite sex.

In working with students who possess and show pornographic material as an attention-getting effort, the teacher usually does not need to be concerned about any negative student behavior characteristics. Consequently, holding a short but serious discussion with the student usually is sufficient. This discussion should help the student understand that his actions are to draw attention to himself, that the material is not acceptable in the school, and that any further material taken from him will be given to his parents.

Another approach teachers can use is more formalized counseling. Here the teacher, parent, and child discuss the student's present and future, maturation stages and his expanding interest in sexual development. Stress is placed on the parent role in providing sex education for his child. The teacher works with the student in helping him develop positive social relationships with students of the opposite sex. Working together, the teacher and parents generally redirect the student's curiosity relatively quickly.

Still another approach is for the teacher simply to confiscate the material, show it to the parent, and discuss with the parent appropriate remedial measures. In this situation, usually it is left to the parent to take whatever action is deemed necessary. This approach is recommended only if there is a strong family structure. If there is not, leaving action up to the parent usually results in little other than a brief parental scolding of the student.

A fourth approach the teacher can take is to confiscate and destroy the objectionable material and inform the student he will be referred to the proper administrator for action. This necessitates the teacher's observing the student for possession of further material, and his overt actions with other students, particularly those of the opposite sex. Discussions with other staff members on a follow-up basis can very well reveal whether or not the problem was solved with the threat of a referral or whether additional incidents observed by other teachers indicate a more serious problem. The nature of the problem would determine the type of follow-up referral needed.

HOW TO: ESTABLISH A STUDENT HONOR CODE

One of the most valuable documents that a school can have is one related to an honor system. The one used in the authors' school is shown here as an example of what it can mean in terms of student conduct. We call it "The Viking Pledge." This pledge was developed by the students. It is reviewed by the student council every two years.

VIKING PLEDGE

As a Viking:

1. I will treat others, classmates and staff members, as I would like them to treat me. To do this requires that I respect my teachers and fellow students, cooperate with them and hold my responsibilities to myself, and to my school, seriously and with honor.
2. I will respect school property and the property of others without constant reminder. I will avoid defacing lockers, walls and desks. I will make neatness and cleanliness of the school building one of my individual responsibilities.
3. I will encourage courtesy and honesty. I will develop character and maturity through acceptance of responsibility and self-control. I will make every effort to be prompt, dependable and trustworthy.
4. I will do the very best work of which I am capable to bring

credit to myself, my home, my school and my community.

5. I will personally help to maintain law and order in the school and community. I will keep aware of all school regulations so that I may follow them with understanding.

6. I will try to grow away from immature habits, attitudes, and approaches to my problems and make a strong attempt to act and seek solutions to my problems in a constructive manner as a responsible young adult.

7. I will accept correction and constructive criticism with a strong desire to improve myself.

Many schools have developed lengthy and almost meaningless codes of conduct which are printed in student handbooks but have little or no meaning to the student body.

Honor codes should be developed *by students for students.* Each year the student council should review the code to determine whether it requires updating to meet the needs of a changing student body. The basic philosophy of such a code need not change since it implies those citizen attributes that would make any democratic society strong.

Copies of the honor code should be posted in appropriate places where they can be seen and read by students at leisure. School personnel should periodically discuss the meaning of the code in terms of student conduct and responsibility. If members of the class do not live up to the code's demands, bring it to their attention that at your school, because of the honor code, students have certain responsibilities which they must accept. Imply that you expect nothing less than what the code suggests.

HOW TO HANDLE: STUDENTS WHO
CONSISTENTLY REFUSE TO FOLLOW RULES

There are, in every school, students who do not have the ability or the training to follow school rules. It is difficult to work with such students because frequently the problem stems from within the student's home. The parents of such children tend to blame everybody or everything for the child's problems, but they cannot or will not look inward to see what is really at the heart of the problem.

School personnel must keep up-to-date accurate records about such children. The records should include patterns of conduct, health, and academics. Usually, a pattern of conduct and achievement will develop which will show a depth of the problem. At this time, with the documented material, parents should be brought in and apprised of the problem and possible consequences if such a trend continues. The parents should receive all of the information available and they should be asked to help in developing a plan to solve their child's problems. There are parents who will not help the school reverse the direction the child is taking. When this happens the teacher might consider the following:

1. Recommend placing the child in a self-contained classroom that has a strong disciplinarian in charge. The teacher should be consistent in his handling of the child and demand no more of him than he does of the rest of his students.
2. Recommend the child for homebound instruction. Parents will then have the responsibility of making sure that he works with the tutor and completes assignments. This method usually brings parents to the point where they will work with school officials to solve their child's problems.
3. Limit the child's day to include only the academic activities. Have parents be responsible to pick him up at the end of his class periods and take him home so that he will not get into trouble on the way home.
4. If parents are not cooperative, recommend his admittance to class with the condition that student and parents seek and involve themselves in family counseling. If they refuse, place the student on homebound instruction.
5. If the school has the services of a psychologist, make sure that the student interacts with this person on a regular basis. Admittance into school can also be tied into this demand.
6. Refer the child to a counselor who could hold regular small group meetings with students having similar kinds of problems. The learning that takes place through this type of human interaction usually has an excellent carry-over effect.
7. Try to show parents (by your actions) that you care enough about the student to get involved in attempting to solve the child's problems. This is why decisions that affect the child's

future must be made jointly between school personnel and parents. If parents are of the opinion that teachers and administrators are making arbitrary decisions without really caring how parents feel, and/or the student feels, there will never be any real cooperation taking place or success realized.

HOW TO HANDLE: CLIQUE POWER STRUCTURE

Because junior high/middle school students are gregarious, the clique influence can be a very strong force with which the teacher must deal. The teacher must control this force, but he must do it in a way that does not tend to alienate the clique members from the rest of the class or student body. This is not to imply that all middle level cliques are negative forces, for they are not. It does mean, however, that those negative clique power structures must be dealt with in a manner that tends to involve the group members in one way or another with the overall life of the school.

A given student group usually does not reveal total clique influence in a single classroom because seldom are all members scheduled together. Instead, a clique's negative influence pervades the entire school because of what the group members do outside of the classroom. As a result, all staff members are affected, directly or indirectly, by clique actions. Staff members themselves must work as a group to combat the negative influences.

One of the authors had to work with an isolated clique whose primary negative actions were smoking on the grounds and/or congregating on a corner yard to smoke before coming on the school grounds in the mornings. The author received complaints from parents as well as from staff members. Recognizing he could not stop their smoking, he used a more indirect, positive approach.

He called the group together, discussed the problem with them, and made a compromise suggestion. He would not harrass them about smoking if they would agree (1) not to smoke in the school or on school grounds, and (2) they would smoke in the mornings only in a vacant lot one block from the school. The students agreed to this and for a period of six weeks lived up to the agreement. When they began to smoke closer to the school, the author reminded them of the agreement. The staff was informed of the arrangement and agreed to report any violations to the author so he, alone, could work with the group. Their cooperation was essential. Though he had to schedule reminder conferences several times during the year, his approach worked, with the exception of a few isolated instances of smoking in the building.

In this situation, the students were relatively responsive to community demands on the school and to school rules as long as their habits and group values were not categorically condemned. They were willing to make some concessions when they were treated with respect and permitted to make choices. Individual and group integrity was stressed, not negative behavior.

The teacher can gain clique support by recognizing individual member's talents and providing them with opportunities to succeed in areas outside of group interest. This recognition must be done on an individual-teacher basis and only as it is earned since students can be acutely aware of adult insincerity. The recognition can result in helping clique members reduce their dependence on the clique structure for identity and it can, at the same time, involve them more widely in the life of the school. Over a period of time, it can eliminate a specific group influence.

The school staff can work together in reducing a given clique power structure by providing school activities or class assignments that require individual clique members to work in cooperation with students outside the clique. It is important that these jobs be assigned in terms of the group members' skills and interests and that each group member attains personal satisfaction and attention. Some possibilities are:

1. Party planning committees
2. Teacher assistants for short periods
3. Assembly chair crews
4. Custodial aids in assembling new furniture
5. Assistants to coaches in arranging equipment for a track meet

Another approach for the staff to use is that of dividing and conquering. This involves, especially in the classroom, the removal of the evolving leaders from the classroom or activity for a given period of time. Usually both the followers and leaders settle down because of the lack of reciprocal influence. Efforts should be made by staff members to interest the followers in working with other students and participating in a variety of activities. This can break a clique because the leaders have lost their influence and status.

HOW TO HANDLE: DRUG ABUSERS

The use of drugs at all levels in public education is growing at such a rate that it has become the number-one threat to the safety and well-being of all students. It cannot be said that it does not affect all of us because in reality it does. Governments and society the world over are trying to stop the trend in drug usage. Many schools have tried and are trying special programs aimed at curbing this growing problem. A few examples are:

1. The use of carefully planned programs on drug education which include films, speakers, and law enforcement officials.
2. Social studies-sponsored field trips to drug clinics to show what happens to those individuals who get involved with drugs.
3. Assignment of student committees to collect the latest research on drugs and publication of their collected information in the school newspaper.
4. Student-sponsored programs such as "Young Life" which advocates a meaningful interested life based upon Christian principles.
5. Special counseling programs for students interested in helping students who have been or are on drugs.
6. A specially selected "Students Against Drugs" committee and club organization which has as its goal the purpose of researching why students use drugs and how to help prevent prospective students from moving in that direction.
7. The purchase and dissemination of up-to-date information about drugs (through the school's social studies and health programs).

HOW TO HANDLE: SWEARING

Educators have noticed a definite trend toward a greater use of vulgar language by students during the last few years. The trend does affect the classroom in that students who use such language daily cannot quit using it for classroom blocks of time. As a result, there are many daily confrontations between students and teachers concerning this problem. There has also been a trend involving adults and uncouth language, which implies that if parents can use such language so can their children.

One cannot help noticing that girls are just as bad as boys in the use of abusive language, and that when the peer group is primarily by itself that it is sort of a no-words-barred situation. There seems to be little or no embarassment about using the four-letter words, and in fact the words seem to help some students be more communicative. One group of students (boys and girls) who were asked to express their thoughts about this trend offered the following comments:

1. Abusive or vulgar language is not used in all group contacts, just among close friends.
2. As long as the words were non-directive in their meanings, no one would feel offended.
3. It was sort of the in thing to do when the group comes together.
4. None of the group would use foul language in talking with parents. The worst type of word would be "damn" or "oh hell."
5. Girls in the group did not expect any different treatment from boys concerning such language.
6. The majority of the girls thought that more boys than girls used foul language. They also thought that most girls (beyond the group) would still be embarrassed by vulgar language.
7. The group commented about the trend in telling dirty jokes and they felt that both sexes were moving equally in this direction.
8. Many felt that there was some tie-in with sexual thought when vulgar language was used, but again this was not always the case.
9. The majority would not use such language in a classroom because
   a. they did not feel that it was right,
   b. they were afraid of getting kicked out of class,
   c. they had too much respect for their teachers to let that happen.

Teachers have a responsibility not to use abusive language before their students. If they do use such language, they have a responsibility to apologize to the students. In most cases, this will end the problem created by the outburst right on the spot. It should be noted that teachers are concerned about the swearing trends that are taking place and are counseling the following solutions to try to reverse the trend:

1. If swearing occurs in the classroom, counsel the offender initially in a gentle manner, but make sure he understands that you will not tolerate it again.
2. Hold student group meetings to discuss the probable reasons why people swear.
3. When abusive language occurs, make sure the offender knows that some people are offended by it.
4. Involve parental groups through PTA contacts in discussions of swearing trends on the part of both adults and students.
5. Make sure that the problem of swearing is curtailed by "Codes of Conduct," building and classroom rules, etc.
6. Since all people react differently to swearing, try to receive group agreement on the part of the teaching staff as to what is acceptable and not acceptable, and what type of punishment should be used for those students who are proverbial offenders.

Teachers have observed that when they give students the opportunity to talk about it, the students fairly much agree that swearing is a problem and one not really appreciated. The students go so far as to recommend possible disciplinary penalties. They have also noted that where specific teachers have a tendency to swear, the students in their classes are also prone to swearing. One school periodically invites parents in to debate such problems as swearing. Teachers, students, and parents are involved in the debates.

HOW TO HANDLE: SMOKING

Societal mores have been changing steadily relative to topics like smoking. A sharp division is becoming apparent relative to those

, who do and those who don't smoke. One would think that at the middle school level smoking should not be a problem. However, this is not the case. Students today are more prone to be flagrant in their use of tobacco than they were a few years back. Many students at the upper elementary level bring to the middle two or three years of smoking experience. By the time they are 12 and 13 years old, they are old-timers to the world of tobacco.

Parent contacts about smoking problems run the full scale of emotion. Many parents, especially because of the supposed link between cancer and tobacco, cannot understand why students would do such a thing. Many are offended to think that educators would dare say that their youngster smokes. There is also a growing number of parents who respond by saying "so what." However, the majority do not want their children to smoke and will immediately do everything in their power to see that it does not happen again.

Many parents know that their youngsters smoke but do not know how to get them to quit. Some offer bribes such as a new automobile if they do not smoke until they are 18; others try purchasing mini-bikes; and others using love and psychology will do their bit to solve the problem in that manner.

Educators are pretty much in agreement that students, especially those under 18, should not smoke. School rules are usually definite about nonsmoking and many include penalties. Students involved in athletics must make the choice between the sport and the right to smoke.

Educators might wish to consider the following techniques to control smoking:

1. Starting with the student handbook, clarify the rule about *no* smoking and indicate the initial punishment plus follow-up types of punishment (*Example*—the first-time offenders will be suspended for three days; second-time offenders will be suspended for five days!).
2. Discuss the rules and their penalties with the parent-teacher organization.
3. Ask all staff to be consistent in dealing with the smoking problem.
4. When a student is caught smoking:
   a. make sure a record of the event is kept,

      b. telephone parents and ask them to come and pick up their student,

      c. inform the staff about the student and the suspension,

      d. if the student wishes to hand in homework, have him come to the school after the regular school day is over, and at that time he could also talk to teachers about assignments.

5. A second offense might carry a 5-day suspension and possible D's for each day, even though homework will be turned in.

6. If there is a group of hard-core smokers, make sure that they and their parents know of the penalties.

Middle level students often do not think about possible serious consequences resulting from their smoking in the building. One burning cigarette furtively discarded in a wastebasket, hidden in a ventilator opening, or thrown in a storage area can endanger the lives and/or belongings of many students.

HOW TO HANDLE: LACK OF RESPECT FOR OTHERS

Showing lack of concern or respect for others, peers and adults, is one of the major complaints teachers have about middle level students. Many times it is difficult for staff members to identify specific reasons for this student rudeness. Lack of parental training, clique behavior patterns, defensiveness, reaction to adult behavior, and desire for attention can be causes of student display of a lack of concern for others. This problem usually cannot be resolved quickly because change here involves a change in student attitude.

Direct teacher criticism of a student's actions usually will not prove an effective method in helping a student become more considerate of others. The child learns more quickly when he begins to understand the negative effect his rudeness has on his own efforts to gain social acceptance, especially with his peers. The teacher should use the peer resources available to him. There are several ways the instructor can do this.

The child who is rude to other students soon finds he is being left alone. He is generally more aware of his isolation than he is of the reasons for it. Consequently, he tends to react in an even more negative manner as a way of "getting even" with other students. Before this happens, the teacher should begin helping the child recognize the causes of his rejection.

The teacher can find the use of a tape recorder or a video-tape recorder very helpful here. By recording the student's remarks and actions, then discussing these with him and his parents in terms of the overt reactions of other students, the offending child can begin to understand that his own actions are often the cause of his problem. By watching and listening to the reactions of other students, the isolate child will have difficulty in justifying his own actions and attempting to blame others. It is important here that the teacher display a sympathetic attitude, for the child is being forced to view himself in a negative way. Also, the instructor can offer specific suggestions to help the child improve his peer relationships.

The teacher can also adopt a "wait and see" attitude. In this case, he observes the student and the way other students react to him. The instructor permits peer actions to apply pressure on the isolate student to change his attitude and actions. Care must be taken by the teacher to keep the situation from becoming oppressive to the child, however. The teacher can prevent this by having a conference with the child after each conflict incident, discussing with him specific results and how he could have prevented these.

With this approach, the teacher is permitting the child to experience a negative situation, then helping him analyze it immediately after it happens. Once this is done, the student can be placed quickly back into a group situation, hopefully attempting to function on the basis of his conference with the teacher. It is essential that the student understand he must change his actions before he can expect other students to change theirs.

To a middle level student, peer isolation is most difficult to accept. If a child continues to experience peer rejection even after the teacher has worked with him, the only alternative left is to refer the child to a school psychologist for further help, with the recommendation the student be transferred from the class in which he has been isolated by his classmates.

HOW TO HANDLE: GAMBLING

The problem of gambling goes in streaks. Middle level students are not interested in it to the same degree as are high school students. The two factors that seem to curb gambling are: (1) a quiet area, and (2) availability of money and time. Middle school schedules are usually pretty rigid when it comes to time and if a recess or play period is included, students at this level want to expend energy.

Gambling is not allowed in the public schools. Most schools have written rules outlawing it, though very few specify penalties. If money is involved, it will be confiscated. If the stakes are something else, they will also be taken away.

1. Make sure that the rule about gambling, and the penalties attached to it are clearly understood.
2. Counsel offenders as to the costs of gambling.
3. Assign a research project on gambling—what are the odds, and who wins?—to be written and handed in.

Since gambling is not as serious a problem as smoking or drug abuse in most middle schools, the penalties should not be as severe as for these other problems. If gambling does present a problem, the staff should assist in deciding what kind of disciplinary punishment should be exacted.

HOW TO HANDLE: STEALING FOOD FROM OTHER'S TRAYS

Stealing food in the cafeteria, in most cases, is a problem presented by relatively few students. In some instances, the cause of the problem is minor; that is, a student has lost his lunch money, would rather save it, or simply forgot it. In other instances, stealing of food may be the result of a more serious problem related to inadequate family finances, parental pride preventing issuance of free lunches, money spent in other ways, shakedowns, or other reasons.

Before any action is taken in response to a student's stealing food, it is important that the staff members involved take time to identify the specific reason for the child's thefts. Regardless of any follow-up actions which are deemed necessary, measures should be taken to stop the stealing immediately. Below are some actions the school staff can initiate to discourage food theft, pending the identification of any need for implementation of remedial measures to resolve more serious underlying problems.

At the beginning of the school year, lunch rules and procedures should be posted in a conspicuous place in the cafeteria. These regulations should be clearly explained to all students, along with penalties for violations. The penalties should not be posted in the lunch room because this helps to create a negative eating atmosphere. These remediation measures, after all, are written for a relatively small number of students.

Once the rules are explained, they must be enforced consistently. Lack of consistent enforcement encourages negative student action. A spur of the moment action, through staff neglect, can quickly become a behavioral pattern.

Develop remedial practices that can be implemented immediately. Several that can be very effective are:

1. Escorting the student to the cafeteria to buy his lunch and accompany him to an isolated eating area.
2. Requiring the pupil to bring a sack lunch and eat in the office.
3. Requesting the parent to observe his child's actions in the cafeteria.
4. Demanding that the student pay other students for food taken from their trays.
5. Permitting the student to enter the lunchroom only after the other students have eaten.

These corrective measures are based on the premise that the offending student has shown that he cannot abide by the accepted rules of the lunchroom. He has also indicated he cannot respect the rights of others. Consequently, he will eat in a separate location until he reveals a willingness to follow approved cafeteria behavior demands.

4

Improving Student-Peer Relationships

HOW TO HANDLE: STUDENTS WHO SHOW
EXCESSIVE ATTENTION TO THE OPPOSITE SEX

Usually between the ages of 12 and 16 students begin to realize that there is an opposite sex and that its members can be very interesting. Prior to this time most students seemingly just put up with them because they are in the vicinity. However, as mother nature takes her course, they develop an infatuation for the opposite sex. When not carried to an extreme, this can be something very beautiful and natural.

There are students, both boys and girls, who do carry these early relationships too far. It is in this context that we as teachers must apply our skills to help students realize that where such activity is carried to an extreme, only trouble can result.

It takes wise parents to prepare their young for the onset of puberty and young adulthood. School personnel can also help by offering programs (either in science or in social studies, or perhaps both areas) aimed at developing an understanding both of mental and physical growth patterns. Some schools offer programs in sex education, starting the program at the primary school level and adding steps each year through the eighth grade level. Special teachers are hired to teach the course, and students have the option about taking it or not taking it. During the course such topics as excessive attention or involvement with the opposite sex are discussed.

Students who have not participated in any such program and are having trouble in this respect must be counseled concerning their actions. During the initial period of counseling the following should be stressed: (a) that the school must discourage excessive demonstration of affection, (b) that an attention or awareness of the opposite sex is normal, (c) that when such attention does not interfere with a person's ability to accept general responsibilities it can be good, (d) that too much attention will affect the overall performance of a student no matter what task he undertakes, and (e) it would behoove the student to be aware of what is acceptable behavior and interest and what is not acceptable.

Parents can unwittingly start a child in the direction of excessive attention towards the opposite sex by the way they dress their child, by the way they talk, by the way they act towards one another in the family setting, by their allowance of early dating routines, and so on. Teachers must understand that all of these things have been a part of the developmental influences in the child's life. If school personnel have continuing trouble in solving the problem, parents must be brought in so that they are aware of what is happening and can help in keeping the problem under control.

HOW TO CONTROL: TEASING

Most people enjoy being teased to a degree, for in teasing there is humor. When teasing becomes abusive, however, people will usually react with anger and hostility. The middle school child is caught in a point of transition relative to teasing; as a youngster he received the teasing, and as a pre-teen he wants to dole some of it out to friends. Hence, the experience is fairly new. He usually does not know when to quit.

There are also many students who are offended by teasing. These students, like those who do not know when to quit teasing, find that they create problems for themselves, problems they do not want. As a result of this type of doubt conflict, it is imperative that youngsters be taught, more by example than by lecture, what teasing is all about. Teachers are in an excellent position to show by example what teasing is, what it can do, how people react to it, and what limitations should be placed upon it.

Teasing, as an educational tool, is invaluable. Since most students receive a certain amount of teasing as they grow up, most are not abused by it. It is by being teased that they learn in turn to tease. The child who cannot stand teasing faces a special kind of abuse from his peers. They usually react by becoming openly abusive with the individual and then encourage others to join in the abuse. When this happens tempers flare on both sides, and things can easily get out of control.

In this case, teachers should (1) discuss why people tease, (2) explain that teasing is not necessarily negative oriented, and can in fact be a way of indicating a desire for friendship, and (3) discuss the limits which should be placed on teasing so that people are not abused by it.

It is important that students who are being teased be counseled privately, if possible. Even though the whole class may have discussed teasing, individuals who are special objects of teasing must be carefully guided through this problem. They should be made aware of the following:

1. That if they always react negatively, they will incur more teasing;
2. That it is possible to stop a person from teasing by teasing gently in return;
   Example: Ruth, a pretty 12-year-old, was being teased unmercifully about her red hair and rosy complexion, and this upset her to the point that she was ready to fight. After being counseled about the teasing, her reaction to the boy changed and she openly asked him, "If you really like me why don't you just come out and say so!" The boy was very embarrassed and never teased her again.
3. That as long as the teasing is not abusive, it is possible to enjoy the attention it brings;
4. That if teasing becomes abusive, an adult should be asked for help so that the person doing the teasing will be brought into line and will develop an understanding of what appropriate teasing is.

If a student's personality will not allow for teasing, the teacher will have to bring in the offender or offenders and request that the teasing stop. The word request is important at this first stage, for hopefully students will be guided into understanding that there are different types of personalities in any group setting and that some individuals cannot, for whatever reason, accept teasing.

HOW TO HANDLE: GROUP OSTRACISM

It is an unfortunate fact that we have problems in our schools with things like group isolationism. There are so many factors which create this problem that we can only involve ourselves with a few such factors here. Race, monetary problems, personality variances, physical differences, academic interests—these are but a few of the reasons given for ostracizing and isolating special groups of students. When school personnel see this happening, they should do their best to try to prevent its taking place. Students who find themselves in such groups eventually begin to accept the cliquishness of the situation and mark themselves as being different and to a degree special in some unique way. This is oftentimes how gangs begin, and the resulting divisiveness within the student body is very destructive.

Of course, some groups want to be left alone, such as students involved in the drug culture, the less than successful students, and those who identify themselves as being discipline problems. When a student opts for membership in such a group it is difficult for staff members to counsel him through his problems because he has the moral support of peers to continue in a negative direction.

Successful schools have a unified student body, one whose main purpose is to encourage involvement leading to high morale and the continuing development of a curriculum which meets their needs. If cliques are encouraged, if special groups like the athletes are singled out for favors and rewards, if music and drama are allowed to play a greater leadership role than other groups, then a school will have problems with group isolationism. It behooves school personnel to balance the program so that the majority of needs are met, not just a few.

HOW TO HANDLE: THE LONER

The loner is not necessarily a problem within the school, for many young people are complete individualists even at this early age. If there is a problem with a child's being a loner, it takes place when there is a complete rejection of any type of social and/or interest type of friendship. Teachers should be looking for students who fall into this category, and through observation try to find out if the student is secure in his individualistic role or if in fact he really has a problem with making and keeping friends. If the latter is the case, one is dealing with a very unhappy child and it will take some real thought and personal involvement to help him work through his problem.

Example: Many parents, because of job responsibilities, are forced to move from one area to another quite often. Marcia's parents indicated to her that their moves were necessary to maintain their standard of being. Marcia became withdrawn and no longer attempted to make friends because of the hurt created in always having to part soon after friendships were formed. Marcia's parents thought this to be a stage that all children go through as they grow. When they finally realized, as a result of special family counseling, what was happening to Marcia, they asked their employer for a permanent status while Marcia completed her schooling. It was granted. Once Marcia realized that this was possible, she once again became a positive outgoing type of person, and looked forward to being a part of school activities.

A child who tends to be a loner will tend to initially not want help from adults or from peers, although down deep he probably would like to be a part of a group and have close friends. It takes a great deal of gentleness on the part of the person who is trying to help such a student, and it will also take a great deal of perseverance. At first the student will seem to be affronted by the intrusion on his privacy. However, he will usually try to keep a door open with an interested adult if, in fact, he does not like being a loner. Group counseling techniques usually work best in trying to reinvolve a student in school activities, since he can respond as he wishes or just remain silent and listen to the interaction going on around him. A counselor can set up a controlled environment where the purpose of the discussion will be aimed at topics related to loneliness, rejection, and so on. The make-up of the group can also be controlled, allowing for a balance of students from all environments of the school. If an atmosphere of openness and honesty can prevail, the results will probably be very positive. If the atmosphere seems to be false, the results will end disastrously. If there is a point of warning about such a technique, it lies in the selection of the participants. If just one member of the group is of such a type of personality that will cause friction, the total group will probably not interact.

Another technique to help a student who has withdrawal tendencies is to involve members of his peer group in a consultative capacity. These students know why they are being asked to talk with and encourage specific students. Peer interaction is one of the best techniques available in helping young people make friends, and also in helping young people solve personal problems.

HOW TO HANDLE: NEGATIVE ATTENTION-GETTING

Many students go through a stage of trying to receive attention by doing something which is negative and/or destructive. When teachers observe such actions, they must immediately try to redirect this overt type of activity into positive channels. If the action is always negative, a teacher should bring to the student's attention that such behavior is not desirable and usually receives the wrong response. Teachers usually react to negative acts of attention-getting in a negative way as well. Rules are then set up which will attempt to curb the negativism. If the student persists, he might be sent out of the class until that time when he can control his need for attention. Teachers should send such a student to the office and should ask that he be kept out of the class until a conference with parents and the school administration can be held. This will allow time for teachers to share information about the student so that, in turn, that information can be shared with parents. If it is necessary to keep the student out of the class, he might be assigned to a quiet area where there is supervision, such as a detention center, counseling center, or library. The student must make up all classwork missed and do the necessary studying on his own. If this is not done, he forfeits the total credit. If parents and students understand this, the problem of negative attention-getting usually is solved. If the student does not wish to return to the class, the school should not become a "baby-sitting" agency for such children. Limited day schedules with parents delivering and picking them up might force enough of an issue to end the problem.

Parent input is very important in attempting to solve the problem of negative attention-getting. Problems at home can easily encourage students to act up when they have an audience such as when they are in a classroom setting. Domineering parents, parents who are always away from the home setting, working parents, or any parent who does not allow child growth to take place in a positive, loving environment will find that their young people will react, and this reaction will usually take on negative or destructive overtones. Parents must be encouraged to make an attempt at family analysis. Such an analysis must include: (1) positiveness, (2) truthfulness, (3) complete lack of fear of recrimination, (4) unlimited opportunity for discussion, and (5) an honest attempt to change that which must be changed.

Many students who are negative attention-getters have never known any degree of consistency in disciplinary action. Typical reactions to such students would be: (1) physical force, (2) ignoring the situation, (3) a remonstrating glance with no follow-up, (4) isolating the student until he settles down, and (5) counseling the student as to what kinds of behavior are desired and what might happen when such behavior is not exhibited. The child who knows the meaning of limits will quickly learn what is acceptable and what is not acceptable in terms of personal behavior. This should be the primary goal of the counseling approach.

HOW TO HANDLE: BAD PERSONAL HABITS

There are many types of personal habits which are very offensive to friends or peers. Many students have such habits as: (a) clicking one's teeth, (b) picking one's nose, (c) drumming fingers on the desk, (d) leaning back in one's chair and bumping a neighbor's desk, (e) putting one's feet on the back of the seat in front, (g) griping when an assignment is given, (h) belching, (i) talking under one's breath while completing an assignment or tests, (j) passing gas, (k) always turning around in one's chair to talk or see what is going on in back, (l) wandering around the classroom without permission, (m) talking across the room without permission, and (n) poking fellow students to get attention. All of these can be considered habits if done unconsciously, and the teacher will have some difficulty noticing whether such an action is being done on purpose or is in fact an unconscious act.

Because all such acts will easily upset the class routine, the teacher must be observant about them and quickly figure out a means to put an end to them. A teacher should: (a) develop some signal which will bring to the student's attention his actions, (b) place the student where he can be gotten to and controlled easily, and (c) have other students remind him of what he is doing so he will stop. The answer to ending such a problem is in the hope that if reminded enough times in a gentle way, he will voluntarily control his actions.

If any of these actions are being done on purpose, then one must use a disciplinary approach to stop them. Actions such as belching, passing gas, and making sly funny noises are very uncouth and disrespectful toward all members of the class, including the teacher. Sometimes warnings are enough to end the problem but, if not, immediate removal from the classroom will be necessary, with parents being called in to discuss the problem. The student should be removed from the class and not allowed to return until after the parent-student-teacher conference has been held. Since the problem has become severe enough to involve parents, strict guidelines pertaining to student conduct must be drawn and adhered to:

1. One more such incident and the child will be expelled from the class and will forfeit any grade that he has earned.
2. Temporary removal of the child from the school system, and placement in a home-bound program.
3. If the action is occurring in just one class, expulsion from that class with arrangements to have parents pick up the child and take him home until the next class convenes.
4. Assignment of the child to some unpleasant task to accomplish at school while he has been temporarily removed from the class, such as yard work, window cleaning, floor scrubbing, and waxing.

HOW TO CONTROL: GOSSIPS AND RUMORMONGERS

Every school has its gossips and rumormongers. They relish starting stories and creating make-believe situations about students which are aimed at hurting a person's character. Most of the time students pick up such ideas by watching and listening to adults. As a technique for upsetting people, rumormongering is excellent.

Trying to find out who starts rumors is difficult because by the time the rumor is being listened to and thought about, many students are involved. The student or students toward whom the rumor is aimed can try to run down the instigator by a little detective work. However, this is not always possible. Teachers can help keep gossips under control if they know possibly who they might be. If there is doubt they should still talk with the person about how rumors work and how they can hurt people. If the person denies any involvement in the act, one should follow through by asking who, in their estimation, might have started the rumor. It usually does not take long, if the teacher has the time, to run down the culprit or culprits. When found, they should be asked why they would do such a thing. If the rumor is very serious and borders on defamation of character (for example, so and so is pregnant; he was involved in the robbery, etc.) a record should be kept in the student's file showing that that person is capable of trying to really hurt a person's character.

During such conversations, the author likes to use a tape recorder openly for the purposes of keeping a record as to why a student tried to hurt another student in this manner. This technique has proven very effective in ending a gossip's career. The one essential for use of the technique is that the person sitting in front of you must, without any doubt, be the person or persons who started the rumor. If there is any doubt, do not use the tape recorder.

Most rumors have some thread of truth to them. Students in jest make statements which can imply various meanings. The person who tends to be a gossip relishes such information and a rumor is started. When this happens, the teacher must then talk with the person making the initial statement and warn them about their actions. The usual statement received from such a student is "But I didn't mean it!"

HOW TO CONTROL: STUDENT OVERAGGRESSIVENESS

Overaggressiveness and boisterousness are typical actions of many middle level students. Such actions are not usually meant to hurt others but, in fact, students' exuberance can and many times will cause physical injury to others. If a child is continually involved in such incidents, he must be singled out and called to task for his actions. The teacher must remember that these "St. Bernard" types of kids are not usually malicious but they do enjoy the roughhouse world of physical involvement. To play rough is all right as long as the individuals one is playing with like to play in the same manner. However, a student will sometimes innocently get involved and get hurt. At this stage, the teacher has the responsibility of singling out those who tend to be overaggressive and warning them about their actions. A warning will usually solve the problem unless one or two members of the group tend to be malicious. If this is the case, it may be necessary to: (a) take away the play privileges of such students for a specified period of time, (b) demand an apology and restrict the play area for them so that they will easily be under your control, (c) separate out those who tend to play too rough and have them play in a special area all by themselves. One teacher attempting to handle this problem with a group of boys assigned them a special area to be in. She stipulated that the only way they could leave that area was with her permission. After a couple weeks the group wanted to separate, and her roughhousing problem was ended.

If the energies of an overaggressive individual or group can be channeled positively, the school can benefit in many ways. Athletics seem to be the best answer for such a problem. Coaches should be informed about such students and the students should personally be encouraged to get involved in this type of a positive program.

HOW TO HANDLE: THE CHILD
WHO CARRIES KNIVES OR OTHER WEAPONS

School laws are very strict about the carrying of weapons of any kind, and they should be strict. A weapon in the hands of an immature adolescent child presents unlimited danger to many people. The student grapevine will usually warn teachers that a specific student is carrying a weapon or has such in his locker. School authorities must check out such stories and see if they are true. If they are true, the weapons must be confiscated and the student or students suspended until parents and students can be brought together for a conference with school personnel. Many reasons are given for students carrying weapons and most are based upon fear. Again, rumor plays a great part in causing a student to reach for weapons to supposedly protect himself. School personnel must then check out the reason for threats, weapons, and so on.

Most students who resort to reaching for real weapons are usually very insecure people. If the threat is very real, they must be taught to ask for help from adults who can solve problems in a nonviolent way. Sometimes parents unwittingly, by chance remarks, set into motion a series of events which can lead to tragedy. (*For example,* not knowing most of the circumstances which had created a sense of fear, and not realizing how serious his boy was viewing a threat, one father joked that a knife would probably solve his son's problem. It did and it backfired, for not only was the student who initiated the threat hurt, but the weapon his son had taken to school was also used to maim his son permanently for life.) Fear knows no limits, and the wise parent and teacher will recognize the depth of that fear and will try to work a child through to a point of understanding all of its ramifications. Another parent more wisely decided that his son should take judo lessons so that, if needed, he could protect himself. The confidence gained from such instruction resulted in the development of a secure young boy who no longer worried about threats.

The authors' school has a police officer assigned to the building on a part-time basis. The primary purpose for the officer's presence is public relations and an understanding of the law. The officer conducts classes on his own and also assists teachers with the presentation of special programs that are related to law and order. The officer has indicated that the laws regarding people carrying weapons vary from state to state. However, whether the charge is a misdeameanor or a felony, the result is court involvement, probation and/or sentencing. The majority of states do make a distinction between juveniles and adults and process juvenile offences through juvenile courts.

HOW TO HANDLE: STUDENT FIGHTS

Many boys, especially those who love physical contact, also enjoy the world of the fighter. Fighting, if on even terms, is not necessarily a bad way to solve personal animosities. It is only when the odds are imbalanced and someone is likely to get hurt that fighting becomes a problem. When teachers hear that so-and-so is going to fight so-and-so after school, they can pretty well figure out if the fight is going to be on even terms. In the authors' school students of fairly equal size who want to fight are encouraged to fight it out in private with an adult present. Boxing gloves are available and they fight for two-minute blocks of time until one or both say they have had enough. It is interesting to watch such a fight take place without the encouragement of a crowd. There is little glamor involved and in most cases both parties want to quit within a short period of time.

Teachers and administrators must try to keep fighting at a minimum. Our responsibility is to try to teach young people to get along with one another. Students who usually resort to fighting to solve their problems are showing symptoms of deeper problems which tend toward bullying and gang or group action. They must learn to curb these tendencies, and to try to solve differences in a peaceful manner. One school administrator who was getting tired of trying to solve such problems asked for parent support to hold a fight night once a month. Students who could not control their desires to fight were ordered to be present with one or both parents in the gym. A series of regular boxing matches were held. If a bully was always picking on smaller children, he was paired with a student his size. It was not long before students began to seek more positive means to settle quarrels. Parents did not appreciate the inconvenience of attending the fights; however, they did support the idea. Students did not like to take the risk of losing a fight in front of their parents. The main problem was resolved over a short period of time.

HOW TO HANDLE: STEALING FROM PEERS

Nothing can create a volatile situation any faster than theft. Students who tend to be light-fingered are quickly identified as thieves and peers attempt to solve the problem. However, the problem can take on a twist, and peers might support by their silence a student who steals. There is more of this tendency today in the public schools than ever before, and the idea of informing on a fellow student is almost unheard of. As previously mentioned, if peers want to solve the problem they will do it in their subtle way.

Many kinds of theft can occur in a school, including the stealing of clothing, lunch money or lunch tickets, school work, and so on. School personnel must make all students aware that there are individuals with such tendencies around and that they must learn to protect themselves from such people. They should be instructed that:

1. Locker combinations should not be shared.
2. Money should never be openly displayed.
3. Valuable clothing should always be kept in the locker.
4. Unless there is a shortage of lockers, they should never be shared.
5. If an item is stolen, it should be reported immediately.

If the student has any idea who was involved in a theft, the lockers of such people should first of all be checked, and even if nothing is found, there should be a follow-up discussion with the suspected student. One might also check the lockers of the suspect's closest friends to see whether the article has been transferred.

If a student is identified as having stolen an article from peers or teachers, he should immediately be suspended from the school for the maximum amount of time allowed by school law. A complete record should be made and kept concerning the incident. Upon the student's return he and his parents should be notified that if another such act occurs, the school authorities will ask for expulsion.

HOW TO HANDLE: MINORITY GROUP CONFLICTS

Race or minority group conflicts are occurring with greater frequency as the nation tries to solve age-old problems of discrimination and injustice. Schools are caught in the middle of these trends for they work with students from all segments of our society. Generally, rural schools are having few problems concerned with race or minorities since the very life of the community depends upon the complete interaction of all citizens for success. Conflicts are much more frequent in city schools, for even though there is a degree of interdependency in urban areas, they are often subdivided into small independent communities. This allows and even encourages racism to develop.

When minority groups have problems within a school structure, all members of the faculty and administration must work to see that flare-ups do not occur. An understanding of the need and strength resulting from combined cultures must be stressed, and all students must become involved in the process to bring about that understanding. Special buzz sessions seem to work best in bringing about a positive work and play relationship. Group projects which encourage shared accomplishments, such as class projects, money-making projects, etc., seem to work very well.

Group leaders should be equally involved in the general leadership of the school. When problems occur, the student council can help solve the conflicts. Student council faculty advisors should counsel the membership on what the democratic process means and why its strengths lie in unity and purpose.

Minority groups should be encouraged to participate in all phases of the program. Even if a teacher must make a personal appeal to qualified students to involve themselves as such, it should be done. All students should be able to feel that the school is serving their needs, and at the same time they should be comfortable within its setting. Teachers and administrators should openly and honestly solicit, through such organizations as the Parent Teachers Organization, minority group feelings and recommendations as to how to make the school more meaningful. There is no better means of involving minority groups in school activities than to have members of the group working as resource people, teacher aids, and on special committees. This kind of community interaction dispels fears and allows for shared leadership roles. It should be the goal of every school.

HOW TO: HELP CHILDREN UNDERSTAND THE MEANING OF RAPID EMOTIONAL CHANGE

Young people often find themselves unable to understand the changes that are taking place in and around them. As one saying goes, "They wear their hearts on their sleeves." The statement is more than true for the middle level child. Each moment is a new challenge, and has a new goal. It would seem that these students would have enough of a burden just being faced with physical changes, let alone mental. However, the mental changes are as important as the physical, and this fact is reflected in the way in which they handle their emotions.

School personnel have found, as a result of experience, that they must handle some students with a kid-glove approach. These students can be laughing one minute and crying the next, and they are completely sincere in what they are doing. They are in a stage of rapid emotional growth and are embarrassed when they have trouble handling the various problems which confront them. Sympathy and positive counseling are the best two solutions to these problems. The student needs to know that much of what is happening to him is normal and his immediate need is to prevent his emotions from completely controlling his actions.

Example: The student council president was a very dedicated student and leader. She felt that she had to be involved in all of the functions of the council even to the point of physical help. All of a sudden she underwent a personality change, including withdrawal and indications of physical sickness. Parents, teachers, and school administrators got together to discuss the sudden change. When it was realized how worried she was that her year be a success, all adults concerned counseled that she share her responsibilities, and let others worry about some of the facets of leadership. She was kidded rather unmercifully about the worry factor, and once she saw how it was affecting her, she resolved to give her council more responsibility and authority. Her year ended as a complete success.

Some students become abusive toward others as emotional changes fluctuate. These students also need the sympathy and counseling which brings about an understanding of growth patterns. They are a little more difficult to work with because their presence creates a negative atmosphere. They can be a special challenge because: (a) they seem not to listen, (b) they shout, (c) they demand, and (d) they become sullen if they don't get their way. Teachers must in turn remind them: (a) that they are a member of the class and should act like a member; (b) that if they are positive in their approach, they will likewise be answered in a positive manner; (c) that maybe they would like to leave the class until they regain control; and (d) that to a degree we sympathize but that we can tolerate such behavior only for so long a period of time.

HOW TO HANDLE: TELLING ON PEERS

There are always students around who seem to enjoy telling on their peers. This is especially true of younger children. School personnel should not openly condone such behavior, but neither should they reject it. Much of what goes on around a school in a negative sense is brought to light by students who have been trained at home not to put up with such behavior. In this sense it is difficult to categorize them as tattletales, for they help keep the school program working towards positive goals. The author has recommended to these students that if they see or hear something which really upsets them, they write a brief note explaining the situation and hand that note either to me or my secretary. When this occurs, I promise them complete confidentiality. Sometimes a student will tell his parents about an incident and in turn ask his parents to telephone the school.

The student who, in his immaturity, is always running up to a teacher and explaining that a certain student just committed a certain kind of act, should be quietly informed that unless something serious has occurred the teacher would rather not hear about it. After a few times, the student will stop bringing such messages for they do not elicit the kind of attention-getting response that they want. Some young people who have this tendency can be kidded out of the practice just by using simple comments such as: (a) "Is that a fact!" (b) "You don't say!" (c) "Gee, I hate to hear that!" (d) "You're kidding!" and (e) "Aw, come on now!" These statements take the sting of seriousness out of the student's exclamation. Such a comment automatically indicates a degree of humor, and the student must immediately challenge the change and seriousness of his request, or leave well enough alone. Most students will drop the matter at this point, with some satisfaction that the teacher has responded to them.

HOW TO: HELP CHILDREN UNDERSTAND THE PROBLEM OF CARRYING GRUDGES

Most young people do not know what it means to harbor a grudge, for if they are upset with someone they simply tend to try to ignore them. Fortunately, the young also have the unique ability to forgive without having to say as much. These traits allow for the positive interaction for which this age group is known. As students get older grudges become more meaningful and tend to last longer, and finally it almost takes a worded apology to solve such a problem.

Students should be told about grudges; what they can do to friendships; what it means when one makes a mistake to apologize; how to apologize; and how not to make the same mistake twice.

Students who carry grudges to an extreme should be counseled about the meaning of losing a real friend. A few go so far as to try to get even in a physical way. When this happens friendship can seldom be rebuilt. If teachers are aware that such a thing is happening or has occurred, they should try to make sure that the student knows what he is doing. If a grudge affects the classroom, a teacher might have to remove both offenders or at least the one causing the disturbance. Hopefully, the teacher can help end the grudge and try to rebuild a friendship. This might be asking too much, but if it is possible, we should try.

HOW TO: HELP THE NEW STUDENT ADJUST

Every school should have a well thought out program for helping new students to adjust to a new world of challenge. A student's first few days in a new school setting play a major factor in how long it will take him to become comfortable in the school setting. Schools try many techniques to help with this adjustment: (a) have members of the student council meet new students and take them around the building and introduce them to their teachers; (b) assign a student monitor to help the student during the first few days or week; and (c) have the student introduced to each class and ask him to state briefly where he is coming from, what his interests and hobbies are, and why his parents have moved to this community. If each class takes the time to welcome the new student, his initial reactions toward the school should be positive and the possibility of making new friends will be enhanced. The sooner he loses his hesitation and fears about new surroundings and new people, the sooner he will be at ease in his new surroundings and the sooner he will be able to do the quality of work of which he is capable.

One school uses the intercom to announce the arrival of new students and their grade level. Another school takes photos of the students and puts these on a bulletin board with names and a brief summary about the student. The cafeteria in one school offers new students a free meal on their first day in the building. The counselors in one middle school have developed a slide program about the school, the faculty, the program, and the school district. It makes little difference as to what is done to make a new student adjust more easily; the key is that *you do something.* Whatever it is, it will be appreciated and remembered, and it will be shared with others in a P.R. sense.

HOW TO: SOLVE THE PROBLEM
OF NEGATIVE STUDENT GROUP LEADERSHIP

Aside from individual student frustration incidents, a great many classroom discipline situations come about as a result of some type of action by negative student leadership, either through direct overt action by the leadership group or by the environment created as a result of this group action. This occurs primarily because, at times, the group power structure does have control of the classroom. The teacher must recognize this and plan accordingly.

The teacher must be able to:

1. Recognize times when class action is a direct result of group leadership action, direct and indirect;
2. Identify situations that facilitate this action;
3. Identify ways the student leadership functions.

Unless the teacher accepts the fact that each class has a differentiated structure composed of negative group leadership, positive group leadership, and group followers who act in direct relationship to the leadership combination at a given time, he cannot develop effective reactive measures.

To develop effective countermeasures, the teacher must devote time to the primary student leaders, negative and positive, and how their actions are supported and countered by the class as a whole. In doing this, he can use techniques such as:

1. Keeping a log, recording specific situations, how these developed, dominant students and their behavior, revealed student follower action, and instructional methods needed to reestablish teacher control.

2. Identifying primary student leaders by observing student cliques—membership, actions, characteristics, and stability of individual member support.
3. Recognizing the specific incidents and actions that provide the greatest amount of satisfaction to the clique leaders.
4. As a result of staff meetings—evaluating problem cliques and identifying ways of working with them in a positive manner.

Once the teacher has gained this information, he can begin to develop specific class activities and individual student functions that stress student leadership development within the accepted behavioral framework of the school. The extent to which the teacher emphasizes individual leadership development will be determined by how well he recognizes student power forces, individual student leadership characteristics, and the extent to which he is willing to delegate responsibility to responsible students.

Another method for dealing with negative student leadership is the establishment of a classroom organization based on clearly identified group-teacher behavior expectations, student roles in decision-making, and specific objectives the class will work to attain. Of importance here is the agreement on class learning purposes and methods of behavior by students and teacher.

An eighth-grade social studies teacher used this approach, modeling it after specific characteristics each student identified as those he felt were important to student growth in the class. After these actions were identified, the students selected six they felt would serve as conduct guides for the class. The six they selected were:

1. Give us four-week calendars of assignments and due dates.
2. Have student-teacher progress conferences every four weeks.
3. We don't need permission to talk in class discussions as long as we don't interrupt others.
4. One period every three weeks devoted to discussion of student concerns.
5. Plan with the teacher for study time outside of the classroom.

6. Each student have the opportunity to assess his own progress and, in discussion with the teacher, explain why he should receive a certain grade on his report card.

Emphasis here was on student responsibility and participation in progress assessment. In this class, most of the students tried hard to live up to their commitments. With varying degrees, they succeeded. A most important point to be made here, though, is the fact that the teacher encountered very few discipline problems because the students understood they made the rules, with teacher agreement, and had set their own functioning requirements.

A third way to deal with negative student group leadership is to plan classroom activities that provide opportunities for student leaders to teach the class. This requires the students, in cooperation with the teacher, to plan a given lesson, direct student activities, and assess their own effectiveness in working with the class in accordance with specific objectives. The objectives should be identified prior to the students' teaching the class.

In a post-teaching discussion, the teacher and the teaching students should discuss the attainment of objectives, difficulties, and successes the teaching students experienced, and how the class as a whole can improve. Stress in the conference might be, individually and/or collectively, how the teaching students' actions with the teacher in charge parallel other class members' actions with the teaching students in charge.

Before and following the students' teaching the class, the teacher should spend some time with the students discussing with them class leadership responsibilities and how these need to be applied in the specific class situation to attain the stated objectives. This serves two purposes—it offers a learning situation to a small group of students and focuses on a specific activity for which these students are responsible. It also provides for the pupils assessment of their own effectiveness in relation to the other students more than in relation to the teacher.

In one school having a significant number of students coming from a lower socioeconomic area, the teachers had to deal with small student cliques in which negative leadership was assumed at various times by different members of each group. In working to reduce this negativism, the staff suggested the following approaches:

1. Individual or small group counseling in the developing stages of such groups is of the utmost importance. Potential leaders should be identified and via personal encouragement they should be counseled to direct their talents in a positive way. Many such leaders have the potential to be excellent athletes, and coaches might wish to counsel them concerning team participation. It should be noted that no concessions should be allowed relative to their participation, for this type of favoritism can easily destroy the morale of the team.
2. Special programming which relates to community inter- action, such as talks by policemen, firemen, etc., usually has a very positive effect upon small group thinking.
3. If such a group is becoming a real problem, demand that all parents attend a special meeting at the school and if some parents refuse to participate, tie their children's admittance into the school with active parental attendance at the meeting. The leadership for such a meeting should consist of administrators, teachers, counselors, and other professional personnel connected with the school system. Special educa- tion teachers and psychologists would be very helpful in giving positive direction to such a meeting.
4. Home visitations are quite meaningful in attempting to understand student problems. Arrange ahead of time for such meetings so that parents and students have time to think about the meeting, its purpose and possible solutions.
5. Consider the possibility of part-time work programs for the members of such groups and try to give some credit based upon performance.
6. Schedule the daily programs of such students so that they are not in the same classes. When together, a type of negative gang support usually results.

5

Resolving Student-Teacher Conflicts

One of the most important challenges which teachers have in education today is the responsibility of resolving student-teacher conflicts. The interaction which occurs on a daily basis within the classroom dictates the success factor for both students and teachers. If student-teacher conflicts are allowed to continue unresolved, the final affect upon the total school program can be so disastrous as to render any or all parts of the program meaningless. This chapter is primarily concerned with some of the problems teachers face in resolving student-teacher conflicts and consideration of possible techniques for helping to solve them.

HOW TO HANDLE: CHALLENGING OF ADULTS

It is right and natural that as children advance from grade level to grade level that they become more independent in their actions and in their methods of thinking. Even though it is natural for a young person to desire a greater degree of independency, parents and educators must be concerned with the processes and techniques used by students in establishing these important growth patterns. Many students at the middle school level have not developed the degree of maturity needed to understand how to challenge established mores and folkways in a positive manner. This is a growth process that must be considered by each teacher as an important aspect of the instructional program.

Challenging of adults takes various forms, from obvious confrontations to kidding remarks that reveal little more than immaturity and lack of good judgment on the part of the student.

The teacher must, however, be able to recognize the differences between forms of challenge and the consequent needed reaction.

A typical example of this is the case of an eighth-grade boy who had transferred into a new school. He was bigger than most students in his class, had previously had mostly men teachers, and generally had his own way at home because his father was a salesman and away from home three days each week.

When he first came to his last period science class, his teacher, a woman, greeted him, introduced him to his classmates, then, privately, asked him to stay briefly after school and she would explain to him the class work and class organization. He received this as "trying to tell me what to do." He spent his first class period pointedly ignoring the teacher. At the end of this period, the teacher ignored his behavior and explained the work and class rules and procedures to him. He listened passively, saying nothing during the entire conference.

The next meeting, in addition to ignoring the teacher, he started making noises when the teacher was talking. This was a clear example of his challenging the teacher. She could not let this continue. She immediately took four steps.

1. She isolated the boy in an adjoining room where she could see him but he could not see other students
2. She made arrangements to meet with the boy, his mother, and counselor the next morning
3. She clearly and firmly told the boy and his mother the conduct expected of him and what consequences any violations would bring about
4. She, at all times, revealed a role of command, pointedly avoiding a parental role.

The next day, this boy attempted his disturbances. Immediately, the teacher did exactly what she told him she would do

1. Isolated him and totally ignored him
2. After school, asked another student to explain to him what was discussed in class.

The student soon was allowed to return to class because he had learned his actions were causing his isolation. The teacher was going to be firm, consistent, and back her words with immediate action. He also began to understand that other students would help him but only within the limits of expected classroom behavior.

The process of challenge is an educator's delight, for it is in this area that his training in the learning-growth process comes to fulfillment. Following are a few ideas concerning challenge which teachers might wish to consider:

1. Recognize that challenge is a natural part of the growing-up process.
2. Discuss with your classes, at the beginning of each term, the general rules and regulations of expected student behavior.
3. Encourage students to challenge in a positive manner, respecting the rights of all members of the class.
4. As class rules and regulations are developed, post a list of them on a bulletin board where all members can read them at their leisure.
5. For students who are having trouble developing an accepted behavioral pattern for challenge: (a) counsel them about expectations; (b) use a warning system, but once established be consistent with its use; (c) if necessary, use a disciplinary technique such as specific classroom placement, detentions, extra work, physical work, and or separation from the class.

HOW TO HANDLE: REFUSAL TO RECOGNIZE TEACHER AUTHORITY

Some students have trouble recognizing the role and need for teacher authority. This difficulty is usually related to home problems paralleling parent authority problems or adult authority in general. Frequently adults automatically assume that by just being an adult their authority is absolute and whatever they say goes! However, being an adult without a sense of maturity concerning respect toward others, young, peer, or older, leads to the development of many problems related to teaching of children. Most teachers expect and receive respect from students not only because they are teachers, but also because they are secure mature adults. However, there are a few teachers who undermine their positions as teachers because of certain psychological needs related to the desire for attention and companionship. It is easy for young teachers to trap themselves into believing that the answer to being a good teacher is solved by being a real friend to students because of the closeness of age factors with students. There is a very fine line between friendliness with respect and camaraderie with familiarity. The following techniques will help in solving the teacher-authority problem:

1. From the very first day of class, inform the class as to what you expect of them in terms of behavior, student-teacher relationships, peer relationships, and so on.
2. Write your name oi the chalkboard, emphasizing Mr., Mrs., or Miss. Whenever students address you, make sure the address is complete—"Miss Joan Teele." Remember that first name familiarity breeds contempt.
3. Do not be afraid to make decisions. Students quickly identify teachers who have trouble accepting authority roles.
4. Establish the type of teaching role *you* wish to follow. Some teachers need to be rather autocratic, others democratic, depending upon their personalities. If you can identify in your own mind your strengths and weaknesses relative to classroom control, then students will not be able to dictate the role you should play.

Students who have trouble recognizing and accepting teacher authority should, when possible, be placed with more experienced teachers who can gently, but with consistency, help the student understand the importance of the teacher role and its relation to individual discipline.

HOW TO HANDLE: SMALL GROUP
NEGATIVE BEHAVIOR PROBLEMS

It is an interesting phenomenon that students with special problems tend to come together for identification purposes which grows. If the group remains small in numbers, schools using counseling techniques can usually help them work through their special problems. Under these conditions, the problems of each individual member are still readily identifiable and usually solvable.

Small group action is identifiable as a type of security blanket whereby its members find moral support without having to give up their unique status symbols. Negativism and skepticism are two of the main identifiable traits of such groups, and there is usually little acceptance of standard mores and folkways. The membership openly relies upon each other for moral support when challenged by anyone from outside the group. Common reactions range from quiet aloofness to loud harangue, and even to the point of physical involvement.

It is important that teachers be aware that such groups are forming or have been formed. They should seek answers to these questions: (1) Who are the members of the group and who are their leaders? (2) What type of major problems do the members have, and for what reasons has the group come together? (3) Are parents aware of the group? (4) Are all members readily accepted as equals? (5) Are there satellite memberships—members who are not usually involved with the main group? (6) Is the group in general communicative or non-communicative? (7) Is the group usually passive or openly hostile? (8) Does the group have malicious tendencies? (9) Is the group tending towards becoming a gang? (10) Are some members more positive toward rules and regulations than others?

In evaluating the development of such groups, teachers should share their thoughts and findings with one another. Staff-shared evaluations are for the most part fairly accurate, and solutions for handling group harassment are readily found through exchange of ideas. Following are a number of guidelines to solving small negative group problems:

1. Once the membership of the group has been identified, counselors and teachers should work together to help schedule such students so that the group is seldom together to give negative support to each other's actions.
2. If two or more group members are scheduled into a class, make sure the whole class knows well the rules and regulations governing class behavior.

3. At the first sign of trouble, privately take the group aside and inform them of what actions you will take if any type of harassment continues. (Put this conversation on tape and share the tape with parents if necessary.)
4. Do not hesitate to follow through the rules established, even to the point of removing students from the school program if that is necessary.
5. Make sure that you share your problems with the proper administrative personnel in your building.

Problem: Students vandalized lockers, walls, as well as private property. Eventually they became malicious toward other students.

Solution: Parents were informed of the severity of the problem and of the worry on the part of school personnel about the safety of other students. After numerous counseling sessions with the students and the parents as well, the students were assigned to a restricted study area whenever any type of incident occurred displaying the above traits of behavior. The students were unable to handle even the restricted study responsibilities. They carved on tables, wrote on walls and would leave the area without permission. A requirement of psychological help was then attached to the continuation factor of remaining in school. It turned out that the families and students thought this was a joke. The students were then placed on a restricted time schedule which required that they report in and out of the building. Even this program was not successful because of the student's inability to remember the reporting requirements. As a last resort the students were placed on home-bound tutoring with psychological support. Even though the response was erratic, this program was continued until a special school program became available whereby the students were on a live-in basis and were given around-the-clock guidance and help. The students became more settled and controllable.

HOW TO REACT TO: EFFORTS TO "SHOCK" ADULTS

There are a thousand ways in which students try to "shock" adults. The "shock" effect treatment is usually a means of trying to get the attention of teachers for some special reason, even though the child may not know the reason. It would be impossible to relate more than a few of the causes and/or ways to handle the causes of such shock efforts in this chapter, but it is important that school personnel realize that there are definite reasons for the majority of such actions and attempt to identify these reasons.

1. The talkative child, the child who throws items, the child who cannot keep his hands off other children, the child who blurts out in class that he has to go to the toilet, the child who is offensive in language and gestures.

These types of children are begging for attention, and seemingly do not know how to get that attention in a positive way. Be consistent with your classroom rules regarding such behavior, but make sure that these children get the message that you will not allow such behavior. Gentleness tempered with techniques for allowing these students to receive positive recognition from their peers is the answer. Classroom job responsibility, and special errand responsibilities help satisfy the need for attention and yet serve the class in a positive way.

2. The destructive child who destroys classroom furniture, creates special type vandal problems in the toilets, kicks in lockers in order to make them non-functional, spills food on purpose, marks up walls, damages various types of property which belongs to teachers or school personnel.

These types of children openly try to "shock" adults by their behavior, usually expecting to be disciplined but hoping not to be caught. The "shock" effect is usually not immediate but hopefully will have enough effect to bring about new rules, or at least some type of group punishment. To be the doer of such antics is to receive proper recognition from the group. This type of problem can end up in a cops-and-robbers type of game. It is important that teachers and administrators quickly identify the offending child or children, for with each act there is a perverted sense of accomplishment. It should be remembered that students can also be shocked by such actions, and if properly approached they can be a big help in bringing the offenders to justice. Depth counseling with both child and parent, and probably a psychologist in attendance, is deemed necessary. A rather strict type of work punishment comes in handy, especially if materials need to be replaced or repaired. Depending upon the seriousness of the act, repayment should be considered, but this should be a separate part of assigned work punishment. If parents are not supportive, exclude the child from the program for a while and do not consider readmission until the original disciplinary actions have been carried out. Children can outgrow destructive tendencies if handled in a fair and consistent manner.

3. Bullying, extorting, thieving.

These three items have much much in common, and all schools are faced with such offenders. School personnel must deal with such problem children quickly and effectively. Students who resort to such antics can readily be identified early in the educational process. It is better to deal with the problems at an early age than to say that it is just part of the normal process of growing up. Again, as with the destructive type of child, families should be notified of the problem, and appropriate records kept to show the direction that the problem has taken. Recordkeeping can be a real asset to school personnel in establishing discipline patterns. For first-time offenders, counseling will probably solve the problem. For students who have been this route before, be strict and if necessary bring in the law. It is important that young people with these tendencies know that you are not playing games. When the problem is first identified, counseling, apologizing (do not overlook the importance of this act), and making restitution for items taken are but a few ideas for gently handling the problem.

For students who are having trouble curbing these tendencies: (a) require that they talk with the local police about the seriousness of such acts and the legal penalties attached, (b) provide small group counseling with peers in attendance, (c) set some type of work detention which will keep these students busy until all other students have had time to return to their homes, (d) assign research into state and county laws regarding the offence, (e) require replacement of articles taken with brand-new articles, but do not allow the student to retain the old article, (f) provide a work assignment with younger students to see why rules and regulations are important in our society, (g) sign a written contract which establishes the boundaries for such action and penalties which will be taken if one more incident should occur.

4. Improper dress, body cleanliness, etc.

Many students will try to "shock" adults by being immodest, or just downright dirty. All schools should have a dress code which defines the rules for dress and cleanliness if only for modesty and health reasons. These two items do not necessarily go together, although student dressing and grooming trends in the past few years have forced school personnel to combine them. Students can easily "shock" peers as well as adults by doing nothing more than wearing or not wearing what they see in books, movies or on TV. It is a difficult time in our history relative to dress codes, to try to establish decent standards which will be acceptable to all school patrons. School personnel, parent groups, as well as student leaders should be involved in establishing dress codes and rules governing such. Students who come to school improperly dressed, unkempt, or dirty should be kept in a holding area while parents are asked to come to the school, pick up the child, take him home, and correct the problem before allowing him to return to the school setting. Due to the fact that some parents work and will not be able to come and pick up their child, you might assign the student to a special area of the building for the day and have a student assigned to pick up his assignments so that he will have work to do. If the child is within walking distance of the home and a parent can be notified of the problem, the child might walk home to change into proper attire before returning to school. The school might even keep clean clothes on hand and rent them out to the child for the price of having them recleaned or washed by a professional laundry.

Immodesty can take many forms. It might be important to teach a child the meaning of the word, and how immodesty can affect others within the classroom. Do not embarrass a child about such a problem, but in a subtle way make sure that he knows what you are talking about. If the problem continues, share your findings with others and see if the child is displaying the same problem in their classes. If so, have the other members of the staff help counsel, and if this does not work involve a disciplinary type of punishment. Keep records about such problems, for they can be very helpful in soliciting parent support.

HOW TO HANDLE: COMPLAINTS ABOUT STAFF MEMBERS

It is not uncommon to have students register complaints against staff members. How one receives and handles such complaints is important, especially if good rapport is going to continue to exist between students and staff. Whoever receives the complaint must be discreet but honest, and the person about whom the complaint is registered must be notified immediately. Complaints can be the first signs of real or growing problems and should be received as such. However, as with adults, there are chronic complainers and these should be recognized for what they are and handled in an appropriate manner. The chronic complainer needs special attention, for his complaints are, or can be, symptoms of deeply rooted problems.

Many students will complain only as a last resort, and it is important that the receiver of a complaint be tactful with the information which he receives because there are teachers who, out of anger, might retaliate in an unwise manner. Both the complainer and the person being complained about must recognize the fact that there is a problem, and it behooves both parties to get to the basis of the complaint.

Problem: Three students came to the office to complain about how a teacher was teaching a special remedial class. The main complaint was about the lack of discipline; however, included with discipline was an unfairness factor regarding grades.

Solution: The students were asked if they would be willing to meet personally with the teacher to discuss their concerns. They agreed. The assistant principal was included as a member of the meeting. All members felt that the meeting was worthwhile, showed respect for one another, and set up specific goals to be achieved. Two more meetings were held to see if classroom conditions were better relative to an understanding of grading techniques. The teacher became more comfortable in knowing that the problems were being solved and that the hostility of the class was ending. For a period of time the class worked in an effective manner, then gradually the problems began to reoccur. The assistant principal observed the class many times and found that a greater understanding of teaching techniques was needed. Members of the department also observed the classroom and other recommendations were offered. As the teacher became aware of the numerous techniques which teachers could use in making the classroom a meaningful experience for children, the problems ceased altogether.

When a complaint has been received, counsel the person making the complaint to go directly to the person involved and inform that person as to why he or she feels the way they do. If need be, a third party might be present to help keep all parties objective in trying to solve the problem. A third party can also ensure some degree of safety for both student and teacher. If the student has a tendency to stretch the truth, tape the conversation. To keep an accurate record of what is said is one of the best ways to ensure honesty on the part of the complainer, for when statements are once made they cannot later be denied or twisted as to meaning.

Often a person voicing a complaint has need to talk with someone in a confidential way. This is a good time to be a listener, for much insight can be gained by just letting a student "unload" his problems. The teacher can help by:

1. Being sympathetic.
2. Providing suggestions for alternative actions by the student.
3. Helping the student see the effects of his actions.
4. Helping the student identify some specific objectives he can achieve to solve the problems.
5. Helping the the student talk in terms of how he can help prevent recurrence of the problem.

HOW TO HANDLE: ATTEMPTS TO GET EVEN

There are a myriad of ways in which students try to get even with staff members when they feel they have been treated in an unfair manner. Due to the fact that each teacher must teach approximately 180 students every day, it is impossible at times to know when feelings have been hurt or when students might feel slighted. The wise teacher can detect subtle changes in student behavior and head off many possible problems. However, even the best intentioned teacher will sometimes offend without realizing what has happened. It is also important for teachers to realize that there are students who seemingly do not need reasons for "trying to get even with a teacher." To dislike, to envy, to be jealous, to take up another student's problems, all of these are cause enough to try to get even. When a teacher grades a student, assigns a desk, does not call upon a student who has the answer, walks by the student in the hall without saying hello, disciplines a student, telephones a parent about a problem which the student is having in the class—all can be reason enough for a student to act in an overt way toward the teacher or toward the school. Teachers must be aware of the fact that students, in their humanness, may react in varying ways to varying situations. However, one of the interesting facets of being a teacher is being able to cope with these daily types of problems without letting them be a real burden.

In most cases, student attempts to even the score with a teacher are of a temporary nature. This is a characteristic related to student sensitiveness and to the general tendency for pre and early adolescents to respond to a friendly, sincere teacher attitude. It is important, then, for the teacher to respond in a quiet, unemotional manner to student attempts to get even. This involves teacher action emphasis on:

1. A positive approach (the defensive student normally expects a negative approach).
2. The fact that most students really want teacher approval.
3. A remedial approach that is more concerned with future student behavior than past actions.
4. Teacher-revealed respect and concern for the individual student as well as for the effect of any negative student act.

Teachers should be aware of students who are subtle in their actions toward getting even. Filthy notes, graffiti, taking desks apart so that they will fall apart when used by others, pranks which delay general classroom routine—all are ways used by disturbed students to tell teachers that they have problems with which they cannot cope. The wise teacher will know that these are ways of acting out problems, and will do certain things relative to classroom routine which will curb such tendencies from the very beginning. Following are a few of the controls which can automatically be built into classroom routine:

1. Assigned seating with no changes allowed without permission.
2. Student monitors who will assume specific tasks which allow most students to remain in their assigned seats during the regular class period.
3. Arrangement of the class in such a manner that you always have eye control.
4. Moving about so that you know what is going on in all areas of the classroom.

If you have to leave the classroom, inform the students that you expect them to behave themselves, and if you find that they cannot handle this, exact a penalty which will involve the whole class. In the future, the students who tried to create problems will probably be coerced by their peers to behave. The classroom grapevine will probably let you know who the offenders are. Try to handle such students gently and in a counseling fashion at first. Most students will let you know immediately what is bothering them. No matter how trifling the reason may be, be subtle and sincere in your response. On the other hand, if the reason has merit, be sympathetic and understanding. Help the child to understand your thoughts and your actions.

HOW TO CONTROL: RESENTFULNESS
OF TEACHERS' SO-CALLED PARENTAL AUTHORITY

To be a teacher is to assume the varying roles of adult, leader, and parent. Many students resent the fact that teachers can and do assume disciplinary roles which usually only parents have the right to enforce. Statements such as (1) "You have no right to spank me," (2) "You can't make me serve detention time," (3) "Just try to make me clean up that mess," (4) "I can wear this outfit if I want to," (5) "I'm late, so what," (6) "The rules say that as long as I am off the school grounds you have no authority over me," (7) "You enjoy making up and enforcing rules," or (8) "My Dad uses that word, so can I," all indicate resentment towards the fact that teachers do assume adult, parent authority roles. When such challenges are made by students, and as long as the challenge is not obnoxious, a teacher can assume that the student is only flaunting his increasing sense of independency and is not necessarily aiming his negativism toward any one person. However, when the challenge takes on the form of being obnoxious and disgusting, the teacher will have to bring the student back into line and later on attempt to find out why the aggressive conduct is being displayed. An immediate disciplinary action might be necessary in order to solve the immediate problem. A verbal reprimand, demand for an immediate apology, assignment of an unpleasant task, or temporary removal from the classroom are techniques which can be used to make the offender think twice the next time around.

Challenges toward teachers' authority are usually aimed at the more basic rules which govern an educational institution. Rules such as dress codes, bus regulations, general classroom rules, hallway rules, and lunchroom rules create a type of challenge activity. All of these rules should parallel the basic rules which govern home life. How wisely a teacher solves such challenges is indicative of the acceptance of the rule within the home setting. Rules should be made which can be applied to all students, and they should be fair and enforceable.

It should be noted that there are teachers who could not function without the parental authority factor. Such teachers are in constant jeopardy because strict discipline, almost to the point of bullying or ruling by fear, is the fine line between success or failure. If such teachers would accept the fact that students expect and want to be disciplined, rather than to be disciplined for discipline's sake, they would be at ease with the growing up process and with the classroom routine which uses a sense of discipline to put young people at ease so that they can do their very best. If students are not disciplined, they will use every means at their disposal to get rid of that teacher who cannot control students in a classroom setting. Initially students will be subtle in telling others that a classroom has a problem, but as time passes the subtleness will become direct confrontation.

The key to solving the teachers' so-called parental authority factor lies within teacher conduct. Most adults convey a sense of love along with authority. They encourage rather than demand. They retain the role of adult and encourage the young to act accordingly. They do not establish rules just for the sake of having rules, but start with no rules and add or initiate rules when students are not mature enough to handle specific situations.

Teachers understand the close relationship between home and school. Both institutions have the same goal for young people, and that goal is preparing them to live in our society and be successful citizens. The teacher then must convey to all students that there is little or no separation in our dual role of parent and teacher; there shouldn't be, for our purposes coincide. However, our profession demands that we use our special training to help make the educational process palatable and meaningful for all who come under our jurisdiction.

It is frequently easy for the teacher who is also a parent to lapse into his parental role in dealing with students.

An English teacher had to fight this tendency as he worked with a ninth-grade student who was quick to learn but had little self-discipline. He had to be kept busy or he would disturb other students. He was quick to take advantage of any laxness in planning on the part of the teacher.

In analyzing the situation, the teacher decided that the causes of the problem were:

1. The boy lacked self-direction.
2. He thrived on attention.
3. He finished his lessons more quickly than other students, but was careless in his work.

To solve the problem, the teacher:

1. Determined the primary interests of the child and developed independent study activities around these interests.

2. Gave him some room custodial responsibilities, and consequent recognition.
3. Helped the student develop personal performance objectives—that were his own—in terms of class objectives.

This student was kept busy, received attention, and at the same time, felt he was making decisions about his own work. He was "being treated with some respect," as he phrased it. Here, respect served as a motivational factor.

Especially in working with pre and early adolescents, the teacher needs to keep in mind that his actions are subject to student interpretation in terms of teacher functioning consistency, parental-teaching action parallels, and adult agressiveness. The middle level child often feels he should be respected, and therefore reasoned with, rather than always being subjected to the subordinate role of unquestioning obeisance.

Effective discipline results, then, are achieved through the manner in which the teacher functions as well as through the methods he uses.

HOW TO HANDLE: CONTINUING NUISANCE ACTIONS

The majority of students demand that a sense of discipline be a part of their classroom routine. Discipline means control and control automatically implies being able to behave and to give one's attention to a specific purpose. When this kind of regimen becomes uncomfortable for a student, nuisance actions come into play. It makes little or no difference why a student feels uncomfortable in an academic environment; the fact is that he is uncomfortable and consciously or unconsciously begins to try to change or upset the environment. Drumming on desks with pencils or knuckles, taking desks apart, carving or marking on desks, walls, or chalkboards, shooting rubberbands or using rubberbands to shoot spit wads, using balloons to create noises, water guns to shoot water, tacks to put into seats, making and flying paper airplanes, whistling or making odd sounds: all of these are but a few of the things students will do to upset class routine.

Unconscious nuisances are usually more subtle or difficult to control. The student's mind wanders and momentarily he or she must speak to a friend, get a friend's attention, sharpen a pencil, trip a passing classmate, kick the chair in front, write an obscene word on the paper that is being passed around, create a situation so that another student will get into trouble, belch, etcetera. The extremes range from pure subtleness to uncouthness. For each action there is a reason. Boredom is usually the main reason for conscious or unconscious nuisances. However, teachers do not usually have the time to evaluate each incident in a psychological manner, nor should they be required to do so. Immediate unspectacular discipline techniques are needed so that the offender is quietly admonished for his actions but the class itself continues to progress. Giving the student a hard look, walking by and quietly putting a hand on his shoulder, or calling out his name are a few gentle ways to handle such problems. Demand that the student come sit by you, set the student on the floor away from all other students, have the student stand facing a chalkboard, or place your hand roughly on a student's shoulder. These are techniques which are rather harsh but effective in ending nuisance problems. Many such techniques embarrass students to the point that they will think twice before committing such acts in the future. However, they can also enhance the problem with some students who crave attention.

Some nuisance techniques are aimed entirely at the physical classroom. Teachers must know and be responsible for classroom furniture, lighting, heating, and cooling systems. If different teachers and students use the class each period, it is imperative that an inventory be made at the beginning and the end of each period. Do not accept the blame for others, for if a team effort to solve nuisance problems is going to work, you must communicate whenever you find anything wrong with any part of the classroom setting. If you have kept a seating chart for all students, you can quickly identify students who have been involved in malicious mischief. It is important to quickly identify the individuals who are creating such problems, and to counsel them through those problems. It is also right to have children clean up or repair items which they have abused. If the item cannot be cleaned or repaired, replacement should be considered, with the student paying the full price for the new article. If no destruction has taken place but the class regimen has been upset, you might demand an oral apology before readmittance can take place. Sometimes it is best to combine a work or academic assignment with an apology. Many students can readily talk but detest work. Do not make it too easy to get back into the classroom setting.

If the nuisance is aimed directly at the teacher in an obscene or disrespectful way, you might wish to remove the student from the room for a given period of time. During this period the student will be completely responsible for getting assignments or handing in work. The teacher should not go out of his way to see that this has taken place. If work is handed in, grade it accurately and fairly; however, if no work is handed in, give a grade of "O." Contact parents about such behavior and keep them informed about your rules regarding discipline. Request that parents share their knowledge of their child with counselors and staff members. Teachers should also share their knowledge concerning a student, for each will see him in a slightly different way and will also handle him in slightly different way. The child who needs attention, the hyperactive child, the malicious child, the joking child, the restless child, the perfectly normal child who is having a bad day—all can create nuisance problems. Offending students, at the moment of an act, need to be handled in a manner commensurate with the act so that they will know that the teacher does not approve of such types of behavior and that the teacher will demand some type of disciplinary punishment.

HOW TO HANDLE: STUDENTS' RIGHTS VERSUS TEACHERS' RULES

How much and what kind of responsibility should a teacher accept in the developing of classroom rules and regulations? Many teachers have a prepared list of rules which they show to the students on the first day of class and expect those students to follow. Other teachers define very simple rules and then inform the class that if there are going to be any additional rules, only time and classroom experience will define what they should be and how they will be enforced. The latter idea presupposes that students have a certain sense of responsibility toward general rules and regulations, and that they will do everything in their power not to have additional rules defined. Today's students seem to respond to this latter idea, since it seems to be in keeping with their ideas concerning rights and responsibilities.

Teachers quickly find that it is easy to make up a rule but that it is very difficult to enforce some rules. Only time and experience with a class allows for an understanding of what rules will have to be developed and enforced. In some classes, rules will have to be well defined; in others, rules will probably seldom be discussed.

If students challenge certain rules, there are many routes a teacher can take to help them understand why those rules are in effect:

1. Take a moment to respond to students' questions about rules, and invite the whole class to become involved. State your reason for having the rule in the first place, and then allow and encourage student response. If the rule is a good rule, it will easily stand up to the rigors of such debate. If it does not, indicate that the rule will no longer be used.
2. Define your thoughts concerning the rule, why it was put into effect, and why it should stay in effect. If the rule seems to be one that a special class needs, be direct and honest in your response and limit debate.
3. At times when you need to be rather autocratic about a rule, simply state your reasons for believing the rule is necessary, use an illustration that might be apropos to that class, cut debate, and proceed quickly with classroom routine.
4. Encourage a class to write or rewrite a rule so that it is more meaningful to the classroom environment. As situations occur which show the need for a rule, do not hesitate to bring this to the attention of the class and involve them in its formulation. This will save the need for an historical deliberation of the problem later on and help cut down on classroom interruptions.

Many students will challenge a rule just because it is a rule. Be prepared ahead of time for such horseplay. At first be gentle and take the time to discuss the rule. It is at this time that one should encourage all of the members of the class to participate in the discussion. If challenges continue, be prepared to quietly remove the offenders so that they will not bother other students. Be firm in this action so that the whole class knows you will not allow interruptions to impede the deliberations of class routine.

Unfortunately, some teachers develop rules to offset personal dislikes or character weaknesses. Nervous teachers are prone to develop hard and fast rules concerning talking, leaving desks, responding, and so on. Distrustful teachers are very concerned about various forms of cheating. Overly strict teachers worry about being challenged. Teachers who are too lax or too easy going do not like the responsibilities of defining and enforcing rules for fear of losing student support or friendship. To discipline is to be uncomfortable. All teachers have the responsibility of defining for themselves their philosophies about classroom control, rules and regulations, and the enforcement of such. To know what one is doing and why leads to a personal sense of security that can be achieved in no other manner.

HOW TO HANDLE: PRETENSES OF IGNORANCE OF RULES

Teachers have a responsibility to conduct their classes in such a manner that students will be at ease and be able to do their best in the academic environment established. An initial part of this responsibility is to establish the rules which govern the classroom setting. Many teachers, especially those who are rather new to the teaching profession, overlook the importance of this act. For many, especially for upper elementary and secondary teachers, it seems a waste of time to have to be bothered with such a time-consuming class routine. However, it must be remembered that each teacher conducts his class in an entirely different manner, depending upon professional training and long standing values related to self-discipline and responsibility. Following are a few of the extremes in behavioral standards exacted by teachers which any student might face during an ordinary class day:

1. From total silence, to where you may speak at any time but only if you speak softly.
2. You may not leave your seat without permission, to where you may leave your seat as long as you do not bother others.
3. When responding raise your hand and I will call upon you, to you may respond if you have the answer but do not be disrespectful or impolite towards others.

4. You may leave the room if you have permission and/or a pass, to you may leave the room if it is necessary but you must first pick up a prepared pass for such emergencies.
5. If I am working with others you must remain at your seat and you must not talk or distract others, to you may communicate quietly with others about your problem until I am not busy and am able to give you my personal attention.

At the middle and secondary school levels, most students will have from four to six teachers every day. Since each teacher is responsible for his own classroom routine, each child must face the dilemma of remembering the rules which govern each class. If the rules are not clear, imagine the additional burden which the student must carry in order to be an effective interested learner.

Some of the most common statements made by students who find themselves in trouble relative to classroom or building rules are: "I am sorry, but I did not realize that I was doing anything wrong," "I didn't know that there was such a rule," "Don't we have any say as to what we can or cannot do?" "I was at the door when the bell rang, and Mrs. Jones will let us in, why won't you?" All such statements indicate that the rules are not clear or that there is considerable discrepancy in how teachers enforce them. When rules are not clear, the door is open for abuse. Teachers must accept the responsibility of making sure that there is no doubt in a student's mind as to what the rules are and how they will be enforced.

Following are some organizational techniques which could be used by a teacher when a class comes together for the first time:

1. Immediately ask the class to help in establishing the rules which will govern the class. Do not limit the rules to conduct relationships, but include items such as proper procedures for writing, handing in papers, homework, taking tests, absentee responsibilities, etcetera.
2. If possible, write the rules down, and when necessary review the rules when slight infractions take place. Post the rules in a conspicuous place where students may read them at their leisure.
3. Be consistent in seeing that the rules are carried out as formulated. If a penalty is to be enforced, be fair in its

application. Do not allow such things as favoritism to enter into one's decision.

HOW TO REACT TO: TAKING UP FOR FRIENDS

One of the most interesting facets of teaching is the development of individual student growth patterns. Teachers have the opportunity, on a daily basis, to witness this growth and help relate it to personal responsibility. Many students go through a phase where, in their youthful insecurity, they need personal support from friends in order to cope with their problems. No matter what happens to these students, they invite open and sometimes aggressive support from friends whenever confronted with a negative situation. Such support manifests itself in many forms; however, the most common type is a mouthy, vociferous harangue. It is possible for such action to take on physical connotations, and when this happens one begins to see the development of small group or gang interaction.

Within the classroom setting it is not unusual for students to try to come to the aid of a friend who finds himself in trouble. If the trouble is with the teacher, the following remarks would be typical of friend-type responses: (1) "It wasn't his fault," (2) "He didn't do it on purpose," (3) "Quit picking on him," (4) "He wasn't the only one who talked," (5) "If he is guilty then I am guilty too," (6) "Everybody was goofing off, so why send him to the office?" These types of statements are quietly encouraged in order to try to distract the teacher from the real problem, or to confuse the teacher regarding the kind of disciplinary action which should be assigned. If the act is deliberate, the teacher should assign a punishment immediately. If friends still try to get involved, put them down immediately with the threat of paralleling punishments. Some teachers inadvertently encourage such harangues by not taking immediate steps to end this kind of involvement.

Teachers quickly get to know those students who solicit support from friends within the classroom structure. Once identified, they should be counseled as to what kind of action the teacher will take if the incident is repeated.

One of the authors called a student into his office after school for marking on freshly painted walls in a lavatory. The boy, having a good idea about why he was being called in, brought one of his friends along as a witness.

When the author questioned the student, the boy stated that "he was just kidding, just wanted to see if the paint was dry, and was just going to wash the marks off the wall when he was caught." His friend backed his story completely, saying he was even going to help him get the marks off the wall.

The author went along with the story and assigned the two boys to two hours of cleaning the lavatory, and the next day turning in a plan of action for keeping walls clean that they could carryout if they were involved in marking walls again. After the first 30 minutes, as the author walked by the lavatory, one of the boys stopped him. The student explained how he had just wanted to help his friend, but not to the extent of helping him work off his punishment. He had to finish his work assignment, however, for lying.

Neither boy was guilty again of marking on walls.

When teachers are first faced with such problems, they should seek the help of fellow teachers and counselors. It is important that all members of the faculty know that such a problem exists and what corrective measures will seemingly work best.

HOW TO HANDLE: CLASSROOM STUDENT POWER STRUCTURE

Student power structure, if oriented in a positive direction, is one of the greatest assets a teacher has to work with within the classroom setting. However, it can also be one of the most destructive forces if oriented in a negative way. As classes are being established, teachers and counselors must carefully select those students who will make up a classroom unit. Sometimes there emerge new types of leadership, some positive and some negative. It is only after considerable observation and experimentation that a teacher can finalize the fact that the total membership will or will not work together in a positive way.

Student power structure can and should be controlled to the degree that it is going to benefit all members of the class and student body. If maturity and good judgment are lacking in student leadership, school personnel along with parent organizations will have to establish the rules which govern the student body and general building regulations. However, if the student leadership has shown that it is mature and responsible in its actions, it should have a very strong voice in deciding the rules and regulations which govern the school. In the final analysis, negative or positive student power structure decides the success or non-success of the total program.

Most teachers can readily identify potential leaders as well as potential troublemakers. It is not an easy task to guide young people through the troublesome middle school years without mishap. Those students who are positive and enjoy the school environment will usually, despite the usual growing pains, continue to be positive and responsible. Students who are having trouble going through the middle school years must be constantly guided and counseled. Problem students need more personal attention and will demand that attention one way or another. How to give this attention without destroying the classroom framework becomes the challenge of each teacher and administrator. Following are several techniques for handling student power structures:

1. Make a point to get to know potential student leaders well enough that you can understand their motives and their personal needs. Use this knowledge to develop an understanding of what it means to be a leader. Assign responsibilities to such students and make sure that they know that you are counting on them to carry out those responsibilities to the best of their abilities.

2. Take an interest in the students with problems by finding out what their interests are, what they like to do, and what they do not like to do. Encourage a broadening of interests by opening doors to professions which parallel their interests (for example, cars and mechanics), and try to introduce these young people to individuals who are experts in these areas. Encourage work experiences in these professions. Students who are interested and have had some success will not be classroom problems, for they in turn will know that you are not only interested in them but also interested in their futures.

3. If a negative power structure is strong, assign special teachers who are known for their ability to work with such children

to be in charge of their classes. Teachers who possess special abilities in discipline and special education work well with such children. If problems with individuals cannot be solved, those students might then be considered for entrance into special schools. Problem students are not usually problems if peer support is lacking.

4. If negative student leaders are malicious in their actions toward the school or assigned classes, they might be assigned to a limited building schedule, coming in at a certain time and being required to leave at a certain time. In this manner, they can be given the basic courses with special teachers who have the knowledge and ability to handle them.

   As a last resort, such students might be assigned to a home-bound program. The public school, being unable to cope with such a child in its regular program, thus closes the general program to the student and requires that he remain at home. A special tutor is sent to the home five days a week, and works with the student individually in the basic skills areas.

5. Try to identify as early as possible those students who, because of anxiety and tension, cannot discipline themselves to work within the confines of the regular classroom. Such students can have a tremendously negative effect on fellow students if they are not made aware of the student's problem in a gentle way. If a child is hyperactive, teachers, parents, and doctors should work together to find a calming solution for the child. Teachers should remember that the student power structure, because of group psychology, can use such people in either a positive or a negative way. It is imperative that young people with such problems be recognized early and that solutions be considered for solving their dilemma before they are challenged to act out their frustrations.

HOW TO HANDLE: SHOWING PERSONAL DISRESPECT

Personal disrespect toward teachers can be shown in many ways. How to handle this flagrant type of social interaction depends a great deal upon what the teacher hears or sees and how he personally reacts to it. Teachers should not overlook the fact that to let such a violation stand without punishment usually sets the stage for a student to try the same thing once again. There is a learning process related to self-control that should not be overlooked or underestimated when dealing with disrespectful behavior. How to handle each situation depends upon the child, the setting, and the flagrancy of the violation. Very few students will allow themselves to be so obnoxious as to be openly disrespectful. They realize that if parents are brought into the situation, they have no real basis for their actions. A disrespectful act usually results in some type of punishment. A school setting cannot and should not separate itself in its response to such an act just because it is a school, for as such it might be the last institution to impart such learning that a child might encounter.

Disrespect can take many forms: (1) a swear word, (2) an obscene gesture, (3) open defiance, (4) refusing to do assigned class work, (5) negative attitude, (6) being impolite, (7) malicious behavior, (8) nuisance actions, (9) graffiti, and so on. All are ways of letting teachers and school personnel in general know that there is a problem and that the student or students involved are not quite sure of just how to cope with it.

Disrespect warrants disciplinary action. The severity of the discipline depends entirely upon the incident, its setting, the student, and the teacher's attitude toward it. First-time offenders should be taught that such actions will not be allowed. If they are handled quickly and efficiently without special emphasis, they will probably pass without upsetting the general classroom routine. However, if such an action is flagrant, the teacher should make enough of an issue out of it to set an example for the rest of the class. Such incidents open up the possibility of discussing, in a very thorough way, how people should act toward others as well as how to cope with personal problems. They provide teachable moments which are important and should not be slighted, for out of them come a true understanding of living in a society which advocates maximum individual responsibility.

If a student is continually disrespectful, a teacher might wish to consider one of the following types of punishments:

1. Removing the offender from the classroom, for without an audience the fun of such actions is missing.

2. Informing parents of such actions and asking them to come to the school in order to discuss the problem with student, teacher, and counselor.
3. Placing students with such problems in a holding area where they can work on their own without benefit of peer support.
4. Assigning detention study times so that students realize that if they are disturbing others they must in turn make up for all time lost.
5. Requiring proper apologies to all parties concerned before allowing readmittance.
6. If the student cannot learn to control his actions, using special tutorial sessions, even to the degree of a home-bound program.
7. Providing special individual and small-group counseling sessions to help the student see why he acts as such and how he should go about solving personal problems and frustrations in a positive way.

HOW TO HANDLE: STEALING FROM TEACHERS

Stealing continues to be a major problem in our society. Schools, like all other institutions, can be plagued by this problem and must be continuously on guard to control it. Teachers can do much to help keep theft under control by including a preventative theft program as part of the classroom curriculum:

1. Do not tempt children by keeping money or valuables where they can be easily taken.
2. Encourage students not to bring large sums of money to school and not to flash money or valuables around.
3. When classrooms are not in use, keep all doors locked so that wandering students will not be given unnecessary entrance to such areas.
4. Encourage students to use locks on their lockers, and not to share combinations with fellow students.

Teachers and administrators should openly discuss special problems such as theft prior to the beginning of the school term. During such meetings, administrators and staff members can formulate procedures on how to handle incidents of stealing (see pass system). Methods of disciplining should also be discussed along with counseling techniques.

Since stealing can, almost overnight, become a major problem for a school, it is important that students know how teachers and administrators feel about it, and also what penalties might be attached to such infractions. It should be noted that it is difficult to have established penalties for infractions such as stealing. One quickly finds that he might be dealing with second and third time offenders as well as varying values on articles stolen. Following is a list of procedures that teachers and administrators might consider when dealing with an incident of theft:

1. Do not underreact or overreact to an incidence of theft, but give due consideration to finding out what happened.
2. Do your very best to identify the person or persons involved in the incident.
3. If the incident took place in your classroom while class was in session, remember that once the class has been dismissed it is almost impossible to retrieve stolen articles. You might wish to hold a class to solve such a problem. Group punishment sometimes works, or at least a threat of group punishment. Peer pressure to solve a problem like theft is an excellent teaching tool.
4. If the problem is not quickly solved, ask for help from a fellow teacher or administrator.
5. If the problem is easily solved, retain the person doing the stealing for counseling and discipline.
6. Do not overlook the value of disciplinary punishment no matter how slight the infraction.
7. Inform parents of what has happened and of the steps you have taken to discipline their child.
8. Clarify for the student and parents why the disciplinary punishment is what it is and how it might vary if another incident takes place.

Theft should be treated as a major problem with special penalties attached. Offenders should be counseled as to the seriousness of the problem as well as for corrective purposes. Youthful offenders can grow up to be excellent citizens if they are counseled in a positive way and treated in a fair manner. There are some students who, no matter how good the counseling or fair the treatment, grow up to be hardened thieves and criminals. If school personnel suspect that this is the direction a youth is taking, they should request immediate help from mental health and civil authorities. It is essential that parents work closely with all such institutions to solve this problem. If parents are not cooperative, there is little that the school can do except to take a strict disciplinary approach with the student.

It is very important that school personnel know who has committed an act of stealing before an accusation is made. If there is doubt as to who the guilty party is, do not accuse or imply guilt by association, for the damage done in this manner might be greater than the initial act itself.

If a child is guilty of stealing, school personnel might want to consider one of the following disciplinary measures: (1) exclusion from the class and possibly exclusion from the school program for a specified period of time; (2) expulsion from the school program for the remainder of the quarter or semester; (3) a combination of exclusion plus restitution of item or items stolen; (4) exclusion with psychological, psychiatric, and/or family counseling as a requirement for consideration of readmittance; (5) detention work assignments whereby certain parts of the program are closed for a specified period of time; (6) an open apology tied with all of the previous considerations.

As an advent to a disciplinary measure, one of the following ideas might help a youthful offender to understand the severity of what he has done: (1) Require that the student meet with a policeman to discuss the legal penalties attached to theft. (2) Visit a jail to see what can happen if a person is convicted of such an offense. (3) Visit a trial that is in progress so that the student can clearly see what happens to individuals who are accused of such crimes.

HOW TO HANDLE: CHEATING

All teachers must be aware of the psychological consequences to individuals as well as groups when cheating is allowed to take place. Unfortunately, there is little or no prescribed discussion about cheating in teacher training institutions as teachers train for their degrees and certificates. Seemingly, common sense is the rule of thumb that dictates what teachers should do if an incident of cheating takes place. However, because we deal with the world of academia, all teachers should be fully aware of the probability of cheating long before it is allowed to take place. No paper, no test, no evaluation is valid as long as cheating has taken place. It behooves educators to plan their classes and curriculum so that the possibility of cheating is kept minimal.

As classes are formulated, discussion about class rules, and in particular cheating, should be held. Depth discussions about why people cheat, and what happens to their image of themselves, as well as how others see them, should be debated.

If teachers are aware of the gravity of cheating, they will quickly be able to identify students who have such tendencies. Once identified, the students might be handled in the following ways:

1. Change seating assignments to help cut down on cheating possibilities and incidents.
2. Be discreet if you witness cheating taking place, but also be firm. Cheating might be an indicator of bigger problems which need to be solved.
3. Be direct and consistent in handling the problem. Discuss your knowledge of the problem with the student and, if necessary, with his parents.
4. Involve counselors in your findings.
5. Reject any type of work that shows evidence of cheating. A grade value of "0" should be assigned, with make-up work as an additional assignment.
6. If more than one person is involved in cheating (for example, group test or the copying of someone's paper to hand in), assign the same penalty to all parties concerned. Students who allow their papers to be copied are doing just as great a disservice as the copier.
7. If a class or group is known to have such tendencies, accept the fact that a strict supervisory role will have to be conducted. Move around the room, watch for cribbing, notice where students' eyes are going, and do not hesitate to warn those whose eyes or hands stray.
8. Share your findings about such individuals or groups with the other members of the faculty, and if you have success in handling such problems, willingly share your ideas with others.

6

Techniques for Reducing Attendance Problems

Discipline problems related to school attendance are many and varied. Compulsory school attendance laws give impetus to the fact that children will attend school between certain ages and that schools will accordingly do their best to meet certain standards as required by state laws. Districts are professionally obligated to make their programs challenging and worthwhile based upon students' interests and needs. It is with concern that we find many students unable to accept a responsible role in any kind of school setting, and educators have begun to look for alternatives for such young people.

This chapter deals with the child who has trouble identifying with the school and the school program, and who seeks to solve his problem by staying away from school or unwillingly coming to school. The chapter also covers special areas of concern regarding attendance as they might affect a daily schedule.

HOW TO HANDLE: EARLY ARRIVERS

Many students, because of special transportation problems, working parents, or other factors, arrive at school long before school opens in the morning. To say that they are left at our doors is putting it mildly. School personnel have an obligation to find out why these students are arriving early, and if the reason seems valid, to try to accommodate them. For example, a sickness in a family may cause parents to adopt unique time schedules; a single working parent may have to leave home extra early for work assignment; other families may have to alter routine schedules due to hardship factors such as car problems, bus problems, baby sitting problems, sickness problems, and legal problems. To take care of children who arrive early, school personnel should:

1. Designate a special area for the student to go to, and see that appropriate supervision is provided. (*Examples:* special early or late study halls, library assignments, student lounges, etc.)
2. Assign the student some specific responsibility which will allow for a degree of accomplishment and personal satisfaction. (*Examples:* crosswalk patrol, hall supervisory responsibility, library duty assignment such as returning books to shelves and checking overdue lists, custodial help, office help.)
3. Inform the student and parent that the school will try to accommodate the student; however, minimum supervision is available and the student must be responsible for his actions and not become a problem to school personnel. (*Example:* letter to parent which becomes a contract between parent and school giving rules and regulations which must be adhered to by student if the school is going to allow the student to arrive early. Times and assigned locations should be included in this correspondence.)
4. Be positive in trying to help the student. Often, it is not the student's fault that such a problem arises. If the student is properly assigned and supervised, he can be a real asset to the school by performing some needed task which is within his capability.
5. Use parent volunteer supervisors, if available, in solving the supervision problems of such children. We have found that a strong parent volunteer organization can assist a school in many ways, and can help strengthen the overall program.
6. If the student is a problem student and cannot handle extra duty work, inform the parents that the school will not provide supervision and that the student must not arrive early.

HOW TO HANDLE: TARDINESS

Many middle level students develop a habit of tardiness. They are often late to class because they spend too much time talking with their peers. At this age friendship can easily take priority over things like punctuality to class. Student tardiness can become a disturbing class factor if the teacher does not try to curb the problem quickly. Following are some steps the teacher can take to help eliminate tardiness:

1. Find out the cause of lateness, counsel the student about the problem, and if necessary inform the parent.
2. Require by school policy a written excuse from parents for excused and unexcused tardiness. Excused tardiness is where parents accept the responsibility for a child's being late to class or school. Unexcused tardiness is where parents are aware of their child's lateness to class or school but do not approve of such behavior, and were not responsible for the lateness to class or school. Unexcused tardiness should carry certain penalties such as detention time, extra work assignments, etc. Teachers should not admit a student to class without a proper admit slip from the attendance office.
3. Develop a system or routine whereby al' incidents of tardiness are handled in a like manner.
4. If a written excuse is not available, ha/e the student telephone the parent and have the parent explain the problem to the attendance secretary. Require a written note from the parent within 24 hours for school records. Refuse admittance if this is not sent within the appropriate time schedule.
5. Make the student serve a work detention period, the time for which is more than proportional than the time lost (*Example:* ten minutes detention for every minute late to class).

HOW TO HANDLE: TRUANCY

Truancy is the complete disregard of attendance regulations. A truant usually has no intention of attending school and is often willing to accept any disciplinary action which the school might take, preferably suspension. One should remember that there are truants who think and act in terms of a part of a day, a whole day, and even longer periods of time. Since the degrees of violation may vary depending upon the amount of truant time involved, it is useful to enact a standard punishment for first-time offenders. Continuing infractions necessitate differing degrees of discipline, depending upon the student and the depth of his problems. Some techniques for solving the problem of truancy are:

1. Establish a minimal punishment, such as a two or three day suspension, but make it long enough to have meaning. The author's school prescribes a three-day suspension for truancy. The administration retains the right to alter the punishment depending on extenuating circumstances. Parents must bring their student to the school as school closes in the afternoon to pick up and hand in homework.

2. Truancy is usually related to other types of problems. Counsel the student and parents and attempt to find out what things are bothering the student. (*Examples:* Students act out their frustrations; parents who are going through the process of divorce, or are divorced; child with learning disability problems; constant failure.)

3. Try to take a personal interest in the student, even to the point of inviting him (written invitation) to your class. Show him that you are interested in him. Give him positive attention. Be firm in your expectations of his behavior, and also be fair. (*Examples:* Most students respond to some type of personal attention. Techniques such as personal invitations, written invitations, peer group invitations help make young people feel wanted.)

4. Encourage a truant's friends to counsel him about the problem and when possible open the door to other people who might counsel from either a personal or professional standpoint.

5. Take a new look at the truant's schedule. Who are his teachers? What subjects has he been assigned? Are areas of high interest included in the schedule and if so, are they appropriate? Must he spend all day in school? Can the school offer a part-time assignment in conjunction with the school day? (The author's school has had considerable success in assigning such students as science lab assistants, custodial helpers, and grounds personnel on a part-time basis. No wages are allowed. Another example at the author's school that has met with success is a program known as SCOPE. Students work with special adult businesses on a two-hour daily basis during regular class time. Owners evaluate student work and students receive grades for work accordingly. No wages are paid. Only ninth grade students are presently involved in

SCOPE. Parents must accept responsibility for driving students to their work establishment and picking them up.

6. Work detentions assigned beyond the school hours are quite effective since this has a prolonging effect upon the time which the truant must spend at school.
7. Suspension might be the only workable disciplinary action which a school can take; however, one should remember that suspensions usually support the very purpose which causes the truant to leave school in the first place.
8. If a student shows by his attitude and actions that he has learned a lesson and is willing to get down to the business of his education, discontinue a part of the assigned punishment and offer a word of praise and encouragement. It is important that a positive rapport be reestablished between the student and the school.

School personnel should remember that the fairness and longevity of any assigned punishment should be carefully considered. It is very easy to over punish and destroy the basic purpose for which the punishment was assigned.

HOW TO HANDLE: LEAVING THE
SCHOOL GROUNDS WITHOUT PERMISSION

Many schools operate under the closed-campus rule. Students who are in attendance and then leave the school grounds without permission (for whatever the reason may be) are automatically classified as truants. School personnel might try using the following techniques when faced with this problem:

1. Notify parents that their child has left the school without permission and that disciplinary action such as suspension will be enforced.
2. Suspend students who willfully leave the grounds without permission for a specific period of time. (*Example:* The authors' school requires that a first-time truancy receive a three-day suspension. If a student is a proverbial truant, an after-school homework detention penalty is enforced.)
3. Do not attempt to chase the student, because this reinforces the attention factor which he might be wanting. However, if parents cannot be reached, the school might request the

truant officer to pick him up, or as a last resort a police officer. Under these circumstances, the student should be returned to the school and held in detention until parents can be notified.

4. If a student has a tendency to leave the school premises without permission, clearly explain the position of the school and the penalty attached, and inform the student that no one will be coming after him and that the only way in which he will be allowed to return will be with parents after the suspension time has been enforced.

5. If the parents and the school authorities cannot keep the student in a school situation, the juvenile authorities should be notified and court action should follow.

6. If the problem cannot be solved in a positive manner, a school district might request special tutoring for such a student on a home-bound basis.

HOW TO: HELP STUDENTS WHO ARE CHRONIC COMPLAINERS OF ILLNESS

Many students use sickness as a means of justifying absenteeism from school or special classes. Headaches, toothaches, stomach-aches, sore muscles—all are used as reasons for leaving the classroom and reporting into the infirmary. Quite often the student who constantly complains of minor illnesses is using the "sick" technique to avoid facing some unpleasant situation or task. School personnel need to view this as a discipline situation, though relatively speaking, it is a passive one involving no direct challenge to instructional authority. Generally the teacher allows the student some success here because he is in doubt as to whether the student's complaint is valid. Individual staff members can effectively curb this type of student action in several ways:

1. Require students who have a tendency to be sick to have a medical examination, the report from which would become a part of the student's permanent record file. If there is a problem, faculty members should be notified and appropriate consideration should be given.

2. Counsel the child and attempt to find underlying causes which might be causing the child to reach for excuses to miss school or special classes.

3. Meet with the child's parents to discuss the problems which a student is facing.

4. Gently encourage the child to attend classes even though he claims to be ill. Familiarity with a class and classmates can often dispel fear or anxiety.

5. Offer the possibility of changing the student's schedule. See how he reacts, for this can be a real eye-opener regarding parts of the school program. If necessary, change a part of the student's schedule to find out whether or not it alleviates some of the anxiety.

6. Young girls will often overreact to their menstrual period in order to receive attention and also to prove in a rather indirect way that they are now young women in a physical sense. Be gentle in counseling this problem of physical development. It should be stressed that a certain amount of physical discomfort is human and natural. School nurses using audiovisual aids and their professional knowledge do an excellent job of educating young women about their physical and mental growth.

7. Assign students who complain a great deal about physical ailments to classes such as biology, which go into some detail about human growth patterns and the physical problems which all humans might be faced with as they go through life.

HOW TO: HELP THE CHILD WHO IS BULLIED

Every school has its bully. Bullies can make life pretty miserable for peers and smaller students. Attendance can be directly affected by the actions of a bully. Individuals and even small groups of students will not come to school if a bully is harassing them. The following approaches usually work in solving the problem of the bully:

1. Attempt to find out the reasons underlying such actions, and then handle the problem accordingly. Many young people become bullies because they are raised in an environment where fighting is common. Sometimes size alone creates a bully, but often the bully would not exist if it were not for gang action.

2. Whether a bully operates as an individual or as a member of the gang, bring him to task for his actions. A bully does not

usually become a bully overnight. Educators should be on the lookout for students with such tendencies and counseling should begin as early as possible with parents involved.

3. If counseling does not work, restrict students who have such tendencies as to the times they can come to school and leave the school premises.

4. If parent support is not forthcoming, request a court order limiting the student's activities as they relate to the school program and the comings and goings of student personnel.

5. Reach for special programs whereby the student's energies are utilized in a positive way and where in fact the possibilities of student confrontations are limited. Special work programs, limited day schedules, and home-bound tutoring are excellent examples.

6. Restrict the student through use of a detention system, thus allowing other students to return to their homes without fear. A bully usually must have the support of members of his peer group in order for him to perform. A special schedule sometimes solves this problem.

7. Bullying and extortion usually go together. A strict penalty for such actions is usually warranted. Notifying the police of such actions is usually the best way to head off serious problems later on. Parents should be encouraged to file on such offenders so that the gravity of the action will be fully understood. Counseling for first offenders with parents involved and school records updated to include such information is an excellent deterrent to such actions.

HOW TO: SOLVE THE PROBLEM
OF RESTROOM HIDE-OUTS

Students often use the lavatories as hide-outs in order to keep from attending class. For the middle school student, the lavatory can serve as a psychological sexual type of outlet. Whether it is just a hide-out or has some deeper meaning to the individual, the fact is that many boys and girls seek refuge in these periodically supervised areas, requiring the professional staff to seek them out and make sure that they get to their proper class assignments.

1. Students who tend to congregate in the lavatories should be counseled as to the numerous meanings behind such actions. (*Examples:* escapism, knowing that most teachers will not go looking for students in the lavatory areas; sexuality as related to body functions, graffiti, etc.) Those students who use the lavatory as a convenient place to meet friends should be reminded of its basic purpose and be encouraged to meet in more proper surroundings.

2. Due to the fact that the lavatory is considered a rather personal-private place, offenders who despoil its purpose should be put in charge of such an area and not permitted to leave the building until it has been properly cleaned and inspected.

3. Offenders who hide in lavatories should be disciplined via the penalties which are used for tardy students and truants.

4. Lavatories, because of the closure factor, are also used as smoking rooms. Middle schools do not allow students to smoke in the buildings or on the grounds. If a student is found smoking he should be disciplined immediately. The school should have specific penalties for students who are caught smoking. A couple of days suspension for initial offenders and even more exacting punishments for second or third time offenders are not unusual. (The authors' school does not allow students to smoke anywhere on the grounds. Teachers are asked to periodically check the lavatories closest to their rooms. Offenders are suspended for two days.) It is interesting to note that many schools are becoming more lenient toward smokers.

5. Problem lavatories might be temporarily closed, forcing students to use the more easily supervised areas.

6. Older student monitors can effectively help supervise lavatories.

HOW TO: SOLVE THE PROBLEM
OF LOCKERS AND ATTENDANCE

Students must have some place to store their belongings after arriving at school. Lockers are the most common type of storage facility used by schools, although some institutions use trays and/or assigned clothes hangers-baskets for the storing of personal materials. Wherever personal belongings are stored, theft or playful hiding of such items will take place. The problem of supervising these areas is a never-ending task. A few suggestions for keeping problems to a minimum are:

1. Assign problem students to areas where lockers are closely supervised.
2. Make sure that all lockers have locks and whenever students are found to be playing with the locks, assign either work details or detentions for first offenses.
3. Hall control and locker control are synonymous. Identify students found loitering in the halls, especially around certain locker areas, warn them about being tardy, and send them immediately to class. If the problem continues, send the student or students to the appropriate administrator for disciplinary action.
4. Be gentle but firm in seeing that students quickly move on to classes. Most problems related to group loitering can be solved by gentle persuasion.
5. If conditions are crowded, try half-day schedules to keep locker traffic to a minimum. Have students pick up materials for half of the day in the morning and, after lunch, return to pick up books and materials for afternoon classes.
6. If theft or vandalism has taken place in lockers, attempt to find the guilty party quickly. First offenses of theft or vandalism warrant parent counseling as well as special disciplinary punishment. Such a problem should be handled gently but firmly. It is important that the offender realize the gravity of his act.
7. Periodically check lockers for neatness and cleanliness. When a poor housekeeper has been found, make sure that he understands what standards you wish the class to maintain. Counseling usually solves the problem. If the problem continues, keep the student after school for clean-out purposes. This should be done on a surprise basis, so that a habit of cleanliness will develop.

8. Provide adequate hall supervision to check vandalism. Require offenders to pay for damage and, possibly, take away locker privileges. When a student is requested to pay for damages, parents will usually pay but the penalty may not deter the student from committing the offense again. A double penalty which includes personal hardship usually solves the problem in this case. Second offenses warrant suspension and maybe expulsion.

Lockers can also serve as a picking-up point for various commodities not wanted in the school. Alcoholic beverages, cigarettes, drugs, pornography, and candy are items which might be brought to school for sale to other students. Surprise locker checks usually deter such actions. It is important that *all* lockers be checked in order to solve this problem. Offenders (depending on the items being sold) should be properly punished. State laws forbid the sale of items by private individuals on school grounds. All such items should be confiscated. Gentle counseling with first-time offenders and minor punishments (candy and gum sales, for example) should be exacted. The sale of alcohol and drugs can involve parents and police.

HOW TO: TEACH A STUDENT TO ARRIVE AT CLASS WITH THE PROPER EDUCATIONAL TOOLS

Much class time is wasted by students who forget to bring their books, homework, and pencils to class. These students are proverbial borrowers and wasters of others' time. The class must wait, and seemingly the more responsible students and the teachers must accommodate their little game. These students usually wish to return to their lockers or to the place where the lost or forgotten item might be stored. To solve such problems:

1. Treat first-time offenders gently but firmly, for such things can happen to anyone.
2. If the "lost" or "forgotten" tool pattern develops, do not play the game. Such students should be required to sit quietly while the class progresses with assigned work. When

the teacher is free to provide needed tools, then and only then should these students be accommodated.

3. Assign after-school work classes to such offenders.
4. Request that parents provide teachers with an extra set of educational tools so that parent pressure can be exerted on such offenders.
5. Assign additional homework. Send a note home with students indicating what has happened and why parent support is needed. Request that parents sign and return the note along with the homework assignment the following morning.
6. Provide a special quiet study hall for such offenders. Parent volunteers could assist in the supervision. Students are assigned work if they arrive in the study hall without an assignment. Assigned work is collected and forwarded to the student's regular teacher. A grade is given for neatness and thoroughness. If no work is handed in, parents are telephoned and asked to accompany their student to school on the following day in order that they might understand what is happening and why the school is concerned. Students will not be admitted to class without proper books and equipment, and will be sent immediately to the study hall. No credit will be given for the daily work, but work must be handed in that day. Parents should be notified immediately of such problems.

HOW TO: SOLVE THE PROBLEM
OF STUDENT MISUSE OF PASSES

Many schools utilize the issuance of passes permitting students to go from one area of the school to another. Generally speaking, most passes are issued to students for purposes such as running an errand for the teacher, going to the library or another room to study, or going to the restroom. Student misuse of the passes can range from the user's simply losing track of time by stopping to read hall posters, to his smoking in the lavatory or standing by an open classroom door and attempting to distract the attention of a student in another class.

Any time a student is issued a pass, he is given the responsibility for proper use of time. The assumption is made that he will accept this responsibility. Since students who cannot react in a positive manner in this respect must, at various times, be given passes, the school staff must develop methods to cope with the problem. There are a number of possible techniques a school staff can use.

1. The passing time between periods can be lengthened to provide more students an opportunity to get drinks, go to the lavatory, and pass along any last bit of pressing information to a friend. With teacher supervision in the halls, these extended periods can provide students ample time to sharpen pencils and do whatever other quick tasks they need to do before class starts. The extended time also discourages students from asking to leave the room for personal reasons during the class period.

   The extension of the passing period to five or six minutes reduces hurrying and the causes of minor student excitement. The slow pace helps reduce students' feelings of not having any time of their own.

2. There are, of course, personal emergencies requiring that a given student leave class. These cannot be avoided. With the exception of such emergencies, the teacher can take another approach to reducing a student's misuse of passes. He can, with the class, develop specific criteria for the issuance of passes. Rather than have the student fill out a standardized pass, he can have the student complete a form which requires him to state:

   a) purpose for leaving class;
   b) leaving objective to be accomplished;
   c) estimated time for class absence;
   d) time he would return to classroom.

   In this situation, the student is identifying his own terms of absence, with teacher approval. Any variance from these conditions forces the student to blame himself, not the teacher. In most cases, middle level students abide by self-set restrictions.

3. In isolated cases where a student consistently abuses the pass privilege, the teacher has no alternative but to insist that the

another student until such time as he has demonstrated that he can be trusted to use the pass in a responsible manner.

One of the authors experienced such a situation. A student who had a reputation for pass abuse was transferred into a class he was teaching. The author was warned about the boy's irresponsibility and talked with the boy about his reputation, stressing that the student could prove himself without the fear of being condemned by reputation.

Several days later, the author had occasion to send some material to a departmental office. He let this boy run the errand. The student failed to return to class.

The next day the author talked to the boy, explained that because of that incident *only,* he would not be given any more passes from that class. The boy said little, other than that he understood the reason. Because he was aware that he had been given a fair chance and by his own decision had forfeited future opportunities, he was not resentful. The boy maintained good class attendance, but never requested a pass during the entire semester.

As students become familiar with the school system's administrative techniques, there is a tendency for some students to try to abuse the system for personal gain. For example, passes may be forged or stolen, then sold to other students. Following are some techniques that will help prevent such abuses:

1. Challenge all students who are in the hallways unsupervised, and ask to see their written passes. If they have no pass, they should immediately return to their properly assigned place in the building. Such students should be initially counseled to make sure that they understand the purpose of the pass and also what penalties will be attached if the system is abused. Teacher and student handbooks should clearly define how the pass system operates. (*Example:* (policy item) "Teachers will not allow students out of their classes without a written pass explaining where the student belongs, where he is going, and the date and time of such release. If the student is to return to the classroom, the pass should be initialed by appropriate personnel."

2. Wandering students should be corraled. If the student has been identified as an habitual wanderer, staff members should be aware of that fact. Administrative techniques of

control are only as successful as the team effort which enforces them. These students should be taken immediately to an appropriate administrator who then can find out why the student is not in his appropriate class.

3. If the child is a hyperactive child, restriction without understanding might have a disastrous result. As problem children are identified, staff and counselors should pool their knowledge and talents in an effort to find positive solutions to such problems.

4. Wanderers might need to wander. If a punishment is necessary, assign some type of work detail where energies can continue to be utilized in a positive way. (*Example:* cleaning up grounds, sweeping sidewalks or halls, arranging books to be placed on shelves, etc.)

5. Have a holding area for wanderers. Keep them busy with busy work until the next class and then inform the teacher of the class they missed that no grade will be given for work required. Work missed will be handed in the following day.

6. Stolen and/or forged passes can be a problem in larger schools. If a pass is a forgery, have the student telephone the parents and inform them what has happened. Request that parents bring the student to school the following morning. Counsel the parents and the student about the severity of the problem. Require students who have been involved in such offenses to attend small group meetings sponsored by authoritative figures such as policemen, lawyers, judges, firemen, etc. Theft and forgery should not be looked upon lightly, and appropriate punishments such as detentions, suspensions and even expulsions should be considered, depending upon the severity of the incident. (*Example:* First-time offenders should be required to attend the special meetings as indicated above, along with work detentions. Second-time offenders would be given suspensions, and students who have a continuing history of such offenses would be expelled.

HOW TO: GIVE MEANING AND PURPOSE
TO THE LETHARGIC CHILD

Many children occupy chairs but in no way contribute to class progress. Attendance per se is not a problem, unless the child begins to distract other members of the class. The problem of the lethargic child can run the gamut from that of a daydreaming student to one seething with rebellion. Teachers should try:

1. A team effort to find out if the student is acting lethargic in just one class or all classes. It can be quite an eye-opener to a staff to find out the varying degrees within which such a child operates. Depth counseling is usually needed to identify the reasons for such behavior. Parents should be involved in the counseling process since much of the behavior might stem from family problems.

2. Assignment of some basic classroom responsibilities which have the potential of allowing a leadership role. (*Example:* Assign the child to take attendance; pass out or collect papers; be in charge of support text material; rearrange and tidy up room.)

3. A positive rather than negative approach to the lethargic child. Encourage, do not tear down his image. Attempt a point of trust, and inform him in many ways that you expect him to live up to that trust. If he falters, pick him up gently. Praise and gentleness are the keys to all positive forms of change.

4. Use of special interest areas in developing the child's curriculum assignments. If the interest area is not related to your specific part of the curriculum, share your knowledge with the appropriate department.

HOW TO: CHANGE LACK OF CONCERN
FOR POSITIVE PERFORMANCE

Teachers give many reasons for middle level students not being really concerned about their levels of performance; however, there are few student-provided reasons. Teachers tend to create discipline problems by trying to force students to become more concerned for performance rather than by helping them become more responsible. In this particular situation, the student is the cause of the concern, but the teacher is the cause of the conflict. Particularly in situations such as this, the teachers must carefully select and use progressive positive learning approaches rather than rely upon remedial tactics. The lack of concern for positive performance directly affects attitude, which in turn tends to affect attendance. Some causes for this might be: (a) a negative image of one's self, (b) some type of educational handicap such as low reading ability, (c) nonparent support of educational values, (d) the desire to be on one's own, physically as well as economically, (e) a lack of general responsibility towards preparing for the future, (f) negative group relationships which result in the cutting of classes, being tardy, and truancy, and (g) the inability to complete assignments that are required of all students. Following are a few recommended solutions:

1. Individual teachers and counselors should pool their findings about such students, and these findings should be shared with the parents as well as the student.
2. Psychological as well as medical examinations should be encouraged (if not required) in an attempt to better understand cause and effect.
3. The use of positive encouragement and praise (even to the point of kidding) should be tried by all staff members in order to change an attitudinal effect.
4. Assignments should be scheduled based upon an individual child's ability to handle them. Keep a daily record of results so that the student can easily see what he has earned and why.
5. Grade and record books are not private. Periodically a teacher should take the time to bring each child up-to-date as to what he has earned. Do not rely upon the child to seek out this information.
6. If there is a teacher who has had more successes in encouraging a student to perform in a positive way, have that teacher periodically report to the total faculty his findings concerning information and progress.
7. Many students cannot handle multi-teacher classes. There is much merit in identifying such students, and having available to the school program one or two self-contained classrooms.
8. Assignment of such students to small classes which have as their goal the understanding of how to study.

School personnel should also consider more direct teacher-student techniques such as:

1. Giving students responsibilities in areas where they can excel, such as athletics, jobs, special small tasks which allow for the

recognition of immediate positive results, including praise or special trust positions which would bring peer praise (bulletin board assignments, attendance duties, errand responsibilities).

2. Student-teacher contracts which encourage students to work on their own and to accomplish certain tasks by agreed-upon dates. By using this technique the teacher avoids student conflict because the student is in charge of his progress and the results depend upon his effort, or lack of effort. By placing emphasis on student purpose rather than teacher purpose, this technique helps to reduce student-teacher confrontations and encourages maximal attendance.

3. Holding regularly scheduled student-teacher conferences. To make this approach effective, the teacher must not only preset conferences but also develop techniques which allow for a reiteration of the matters discussed and solutions suggested. By using a playback technique, the teacher and student can readily identify areas of failure as well as progress.

4. Use of the regularly scheduled parent-teacher conference. During this conference, the student is held responsible for informing his parent and teacher about his own progress, his problems, and his successes as he sees them. He would also suggest ways he could improve his functioning level. The parent and teacher would discuss his comments, come to agreement, and identify ways they can support and help the student succeed. In this situation, student behavior problems can be reduced because the student has analyzed his own problems and committed himself to certain actions before both his parent and his teacher. The parent has also committed himself to certain actions and can in turn encourage the student to be responsible for his part of the agreement.

5. Requirement of a regularly-scheduled performance progress report which covers much the same information the student discusses in his oral report during the parent-teacher conference. The teacher would discuss each report with the student, making his own entrees on the report with the pupil present. As these reports are collected, the teacher can keep an up-dated student performance file. By periodic reference to this file, the teacher can identify potential student trouble

areas and plan for them before discipline situations materialize.

In using these methods, it is imperative that the teacher not demand of the student more than he can do successfully. Pushing a student too fast, before he has the skills and understanding to handle the situation, will probably end in complete frustration for the student. If the teacher expects too much of the student too soon, additional discipline problems can occur because of pupil frustration evolving from his inability to cope with the teacher-imposed demands.

7

Reducing Acts of Vandalism

HOW TO HANDLE: SETTING FIRES
AND SMOKE DISTURBANCES

One of the most fearsome types of vandalism in a school is that of *setting fires and creating smoke disturbances.* It is a well-known fact that panic can kill just as easily as either fire or smoke. Students who create such problems are not usually aware of the degree of danger that their actions might cause. It is the responsibility of all school personnel to try to apprehend offenders quickly. The student grapevine (if more than one student is involved) will usually help in identifying those who are guilty. If more than one student is involved, he will usually, after a period of time, help in identifying the others who are guilty. If only one student is involved, he will usually want to brag about his actions, and hopefully the knowledge will come to some member of the school staff.

If there has been a rash of such acts, and if they seem to establish a pattern, it is worth the time and effort of school personnel to call in an authority to help solve the problem. All of the lives in a building are in jeopardy if such a student is not identified and then placed in the hands of professional people who can help him solve his problems.

It is imperative that teachers and administrators talk with all students (in groups as small as possible) about the dangers involved in having someone in their midst who has such problems. As mentioned previously, students should be made aware of all the aspects of danger which parallel such acts and not bind the discussion to fire alone. If a pattern has been established such as fires in the boys lavatories:

- Use any means at hand, including the hiring of surveillance personnel, to catch the offender(s).
- Make sure that all unused rooms, stages, and gyms remain locked when not in use for a class.
- Use a pass system that will help identify students who have been absent from a class during a specific period of time.
- Keep all trash cans in areas where, if lit, they can be easily removed and will not be a hazard to the building and/or especially to a classroom.
- Lock problem restrooms so that offenders will not have the freedoms that go with areas of limited supervision.

If students are playing with fire alarms, make sure that all are informed of the gravity of such offenses and make clear that offenders will be expelled. Fire companies plus school administrators will also file court charges against such students. Teachers might also discuss how taxpayers will have to pay the cost of bringing fire equipment to the building when a false alarm occurs.

The key to solving this problem lies in the area of peer pressure. When the majority of students know the danger that is created when someone sets a fire inside a building, they are in a better position to control potential offenders than are adults. Student leaders can easily pass the word that they will not tolerate such incidents and that they will do their best to bring offenders to justice.

HOW TO HANDLE: DESTRUCTION OF MATERIALS AND EQUIPMENT

It would be a shock to educators and citizens alike if the truth were known about the degree of destruction of materials, equipment, and property that is taking place in the public schools today. Many districts have authorized people to research this problem so that parents and citizens can be informed of what it is costing them in terms of money, down time of equipment, and the loss of educational endeavor.

Part of the problem is related to supervision. When schools and classrooms are crowded it is impossible for teachers to adequately supervise a total program. Basic precautions can be taken; but, if a student is determined to destroy something within the school, he will be able to find a way to do so by observing supervision practices.

Students who commit such acts of aggression, like those who set fires, need immediate help from proper professional people. There are many students who will commit such an act, be ashamed of themselves, and never do it again. There are also students who are taking out their aggressions against someone, and use materials and equipment as a scapegoat.

Teachers should always be aware that the possibility of a student's destroying some item always exists. Equipment should be stored in a control area where only authorized people are allowed. Material and equipment, if left unsupervised, is fair game to students who have special problems in trying to grow up.

Vandalism to the outside of the building and to the grounds seems to be increasing. We might be reaching that stage in our society where school grounds will be closed during evening and night hours, and hired caretakers will live on the premises.

HOW TO HANDLE: BREAKING INTO TEACHER DESKS

What is so interesting in a teacher's desk that students will plan and go to great length to break locks to get into them? One student who was caught in the act said that he just wanted to see what she kept in there. Later on he admitted that he knew that she had a jar of money collected for the purpose of helping to finance a class party.

After one series of break-ins, a special block of time was set aside during a teachers' meeting to discuss the problem of teacher desk and locker security. Many teachers indicated that they knew that their desks had been gone through but that nothing seemed to be missing.

A decision was made at this meeting to never keep money or valuable things in the desks. Locks were placed on teacher lockers (good locks) to stop students from entering those areas. Students were informed that they should never enter the teacher preparation rooms where the lockers were without permission of the teachers. The outside doors to such rooms were to be locked when not in use. Teachers were issued a "Key-Bak," a key retrieve item which will fit on a belt and is an excellent way to keep track of keys.

Because of the damage to desks, the teachers decided not to lock them and to keep in them only those articles needed for teaching. This solution ended the problem of theft and breaking into desks.

Another school built a series of lockers into the walls of the teacher's lounge area which is completely off limits to students. All private valuable items are kept in these lockers. The lockers have built-in combination locks as well as a space for a regular lock if desired. The teachers indicated that this was the best solution to the problem of break-ins for two reasons: (1) their purses were handy to the area where they did their planning and ate their meals, and (2) they never worried about articles left in that area since staff was usually always present.

Some schools have purchased signs indicating that desks and files are not locked and that no money is kept in such areas. They indicate that there have been no break-ins since teachers are not allowed to keep valuables of any sort stored in classroom areas.

HOW TO: RECOGNIZE DEVIANT VALUE SYSTEMS

In a democratic society where public education is the basis for the overall degree of literacy and living standards, we find many value systems within each school system. Educators must be aware of the fact that multi-value systems affect the overall quality and morals of the program. Teachers who are working on a daily basis with students have the challenge of trying to orient all of these value systems toward a singular code of ethics acceptable to all; this is indeed a difficult task.

We have a responsibility to try to develop a sense of pride in one's heritage, and yet if the value systems of that heritage are in conflict with building rules and regulations, it will be that value system that will have to consider change. Special counseling sessions will have to be held with members of the family as well as the student. It should be emphasized during such sessions that the basic rules which govern the school in general govern all public schools. If there are differing dress codes, smoking rules, and so on, it should be noted that they are the result of community planning, and are not the result of whims of school personnel.

Drinking alcoholic beverages is another problem that schools face because certain value systems allow (even encourage) their young people to participate in such experiences early in life. It is difficult for them to see why such things cannot be brought onto school grounds.

Theft and cheating are also problems because some elements of society have the belief that as long as you can get away with it, it is all right. This immediately places the school in a vulnerable position since schools do not want to appear as if they were prisons. All school personnel should be made aware that there are within the school structures such types of problems, and recommendations should be made as to how they should be handled.

HOW TO HANDLE: WRITING ON WALLS

Generally speaking, there are two common reasons students write on the walls in classrooms. One is boredom; students engage in writing for something to do, an aimless activity that provides some small physical outlet. Two, students write on walls or desks because it is a way of expressing some private passing thought. At times, however, students write simply for resulting shock value.

Aside from providing stimulating class activities that maintain student interest, there are several methods the teacher can use to discourage pupils from writing on walls, desks, and books. The extent of effectiveness of these methods, just as with any other technique, will depend upon the skill with which the teacher introduces and implements them.

In one middle school, several teachers tape large sheets of paper on the walls of their classrooms. Students are permitted, before and after class, to write any comments they want on the "graffiti sheets." There are certain operational limits imposed, however. Among these are such rules of etiquette as:

1. No vulgar or swear words.
2. No comments that reflect negatively on other individuals or the school.
3. No messages or "notes."

These "graffiti sheets" give students an outlet for their needs for written expression. They know that the sheets are for their use. As a result, teachers have noticed a decided reduction in the number of times students write on walls and furniture. Also, the students have revealed a continuing high interest in writing on the sheets. They show just as high an interest in reading comments students from other classes have written on the sheets.

Another technique the teacher can use to discourage pupils from writing on walls and desks is to schedule, at strategic times, informal talk periods. During these short periods, students can engage in conversations with their friends in an unstructured situation. They are able to express verbally their spur-of-the-moment thoughts and comments they feel they "just have to tell" their friends.

Providing this informal communication time permits students a learning change of pace. It takes into account the strong feelings pre and early adolescents have to communicate with peers, or their feelings for the need just to express themselves. At the end of the informal talk time, the students are ready to resume regular class activities. Again, teachers who have used this occasional technique report that they have less trouble with their students writing on walls and furniture. They also indicate, that in most cases, their classes behave in a more consistent positive manner throughout the year.

There are times when teachers have enrolled in their classes students who are persistent in their writing on walls and furniture. Two actions a teacher can take in a situation such as this are:

1. Utilize a furniture arrangement that keeps the guilty student from sitting near a wall.
2. Check walls and desks during and at the end of each class period.

Approaches such as these help the teacher identify violators more easily and quickly. Rapid identification helps discourage violations. This, together with consequent quick remedial action, such as cleaning off the furniture and making up classwork missed on the student's own time, and by himself, can serve as an effective deterrent. Effectiveness here is dependent upon the guilty student's rectifying his actions in isolation; that is, he cleans desks or walls by himself at a time when he would rather be with his friends.

HOW TO USE: POLICE AS FACULTY MEMBERS

A police officer working with pre and early adolescents within the school setting can be effective in the reduction of vandalism. It is important to stress here that the officer's role changes from that of law enforcement to that of teacher and student resource person. Emphasis is on instruction and interaction. Consequently, police effectiveness is dependent upon officer availability to students and teacher-officer cooperation. Student acceptance of the officer is dependent on the extent of his involvement in the ongoing school program.

The extent of officer involvement will be determined by how the school and each teacher schedules the officer's activities.

OFFICERS AS TEACHERS

One method that has proven effective is having officers serve as teachers. There are a number of opportunities in the various subject matter areas for teachers to develop mini-courses or short time units that a police officer can teach. For this time span, the officer, working under the instructional guidance of the teacher, can serve as the primary instructor. Within this exposure framework, the students and officer can get to know and understand each other as individuals.

In one school using mini courses as electives, a course called "Cops and People" taught by an officer was very successful because of three singular results:

1. A number of the students who enrolled in the course had at various times been placed on probation in custody of their parents.
2. Many students, following the completion of the course, spent time during lunch and after school talking with the officer on an informal basis.
3. Students in the course utilized information they had gained in other classes.

The course was taught on a positive basis, emphasizing the human characteristics of police, how they preferred to work with young people, and how students could benefit from police help. Staff members felt that a direct positive result of this course was some reduction in negative student attitudes toward authority.

ASSIGNMENT OF OFFICERS IN SCHOOL

A suburban city cooperates with the school district by assigning a police officer full-time to the schools. The officer spends one day a week in each of the secondary schools. His function is to be available to students, on an informal, personal basis, to talk about topics of concern to them that are within the realm of the officer's role and responsibilities as a policeman.

This officer functions in several ways. He spends time in the halls, so that he is available to students for short times between periods for exchange of comments or for students to arrange times to see him later. He is also provided a small room where, at pupil request, he can engage in discussions with small groups of students who have permission to leave other classes for this purpose. His third function is to serve as resource person for teachers who may wish to have him participate in class discussions on a single-period basis.

Depending on the skill and personality of the officer, most students quickly learn to trust him and are not afraid to bring up their own topics of concern. Often, student-officer conversations have served as the bases of class discussions and student projects. As a result of these efforts and activities, some students have become interested in law enforcement as a career. Most students, as a result of this program, state they tend to view police officers first as human beings and secondly, as authority figures. This program is considered successful by both the local police department and school personnel.

STUDENT-STAFF-POLICE LUNCHEONS

Another approach for encouraging more direct interaction between students, staff, police officers, and other public authority figures such as firemen and city officials, is the school-hosted luncheon. Here, a few staff members and a few students, randomly selected or present by choice, host selected city officials at a school luncheon. It is a relatively informal setting where adults and young people spend an hour together discussing topics of common interest.

Interaction is dependent on singular characteristics of a given group, however. It is always well to have one faculty member to serve as a discussion facilitator, to avoid possible prolonged periods of uncomfortable silence. Too, it is advantageous for the guests to be prepared to discuss their jobs and responsibilities in terms of student involvement. This tends to stimulate student interest, questions, and comments.

These luncheons should be scheduled as a series, usually five or six. In this way, more city officials are involved. Also, more students have an opportunity to become better acquainted with the officials and their responsibilities as they pertain to pre and early adolescents.

HOW TO: DEVELOP SUPERVISORY PLANS

Many discipline problems at the middle level can be avoided if the teacher takes time to develop an ongoing plan of supervision. Effectiveness can be greatly enhanced if the teacher implements an organizational framework that is related directly to the functioning habits of the students. The manner in which he develops the mechanical aspects and the classroom functioning demands is basic to the organizational framework. Once these aspects become integral characteristics of the students' operational patterns, pupils give little thought as to why the procedures are used.

Emphasis needs to be placed on the day-to-day functioning demands that students learn to accept as behavioral demands. These are not the so-called major changes in classroom operation resulting from classroom conflict. Instead, they are at a routine level, but carefully planned more in terms of the students and less in terms of arbitrary school regulatory requirements.

Practical ways for implementing supervisory procedures within the preceding framework are:

1. Capitalizing on middle level students' gregarious nature through the use of small group and peer pressure. Through the use of observation, revealed student common interests, and student agreement or disagreement evident from class discussions, the teacher can develop many kinds of small

group activities that provide him a natural opportunity to place selected students in work proximity to each other.

The teacher can group together students with differing value and behavior characteristics, by design, on the bases mentioned above. Especially, in terms of social discussion topics, the teacher can note subtle changes in students as a result of the controlled utilization of student conflict value system. Counselors the authors have known have employed this technique with very good success in human relations classes.

2. Developing individual hall supervisory plans through the building approach to hall locker assignments. Here, teachers assign a given group of students their lockers for the year. These lockers are in close proximity to the teacher's room. The pupils become aware that through this approach to locker assignment, they are responsible to the teacher for locker care. As the teacher supervises the halls, he becomes more aware of students around his locker area. This increased awareness on the parts of both teacher and students helps to reduce locker vandalism and stealing.

In one school known to the authors, this approach was particularly effective with ninth graders. Previously, these students were assigned lockers in an area where few ninth-grade teachers were present. Vandalism to lockers, to ceiling tile, and to drinking fountains was evident. Once these students were reassigned lockers by teacher and zone, problems with lockers diminished.

3. Using a team approach involving some individual teacher record keeping and follow-up conferences with other staff members. This technique can be particularly helpful to the teacher in combatting two primary problems:

   a) Students who consistently request passes to leave class.
   b) Students who make arrangements to meet students from other classes.

There are two simple steps the teacher needs to take:

   a) Keep a running record, by period and time, of students who request passes.
   b) Compare this record with similar records kept by other teachers having these same students.

It doesn't take a teacher long, using this method, to identify a particular student's planned absentee pattern. When any vandalism occurs, it is a relatively simple matter to identify the student, or students, who were out of class at the time. Quicker identification of violators can be made because, generally, vandalism occurring during the school day is noticed by the end of the period during which it occurred.

Basic to the effectiveness of the techniques described here is the teacher's being aware of the types of students he has, their singular functioning patterns, and the consistency with which he enforces behavioral demands. Students quickly learn whether or not a given staff member is aware of their performance patterns.

4. Using student supervision. Here, a given student is placed in charge of a particular area of the room—book shelves, student display areas, chalkboards, etc. It is his responsibility to see that this area is kept clean, neat, and orderly.

Most middle level students respond in a positive manner to this type of responsibility given them. The teacher must, however, be certain that two operational rules are made clear to any student assigned this type of responsibility:

    a) The student is not to take any action, on his own, against a student who does not take care of any equipment or material he is using in, or from, the area.

    b) The student is a caretaker of property, not a boss of fellow students.

HOW TO: DEVELOP COMMUNITY PARTICIPATION
AS POSITIVE PRESSURE POINTS

Clearly delineated guidelines for community participation in the day-to-day operations of the school are essential if lay help is to be effective. These guidelines must be written so that both staff and volunteers can function within them. This involves the identification, especially, of the roles, responsibilities, and the operational structure for each individual if a high level of community participation, and interest, is to be maintained.

Goddard Middle School in Littleton, Colorado, uses a community-wide parent structure as a means to involve more people in the school program. This structure consists of dividing the school attendance area into 11 sub-areas with a parent serving as a coordinator for each area. The 11 parents serve as the building parent advisory council, together with the school administrators and a teacher representative.

The council meets monthly, as a total group, to discuss specific areas of concern, to serve as a sounding board for various faculty or community suggestions, and to help set future operational areas of emphasis. As individuals, the coordinators serve as key people in disseminating information about the school, providing accurate answers to questions parents ask, to rumors they mention, and to complaints. The coordinators also refer parents to the proper staff members for answers. These coordinators do not replace school personnel; they assist in maintaining communications.

Through this structure, individual parents feel they receive information more quickly on a reliable basis; they don't have to rely on secondhand interpretation. Staff members feel public communication is being maintained and that they have a variety of parent talents available whenever group support is needed.

An important effect resulting from this particular community structure is increased parental concern for student behavior in school and the effect this has on pupil conduct. Teachers are experiencing noticeably less long-term parental negativism related to individual student misconduct. Parental involvement in development of disciplinary measures has contributed to the solidification of community expectations related to student behavior.

Another method of using parental participation for positive action is to schedule activities on a somewhat regular basis that necessitates parents and staff members working together. An example of this is the inviting of selected parents to participate in faculty inservice programs focusing on public relations, program innovation, and discipline code development. As the parents participate, they tend to feel they have some obligation to work for the success of the program. This obligation evolves into enthusiasm and consequent positive support if the program is successful. If it is not, they want to work cooperatively with the staff to find out why it doesn't work and, then, identify remedial actions.

Along this same line, parents selected on the basis of their interest and expertise can be invited to attend faculty meetings when a given problem is being discussed and possible solutions explored. This approach works especially well when staff members are discussing discipline problems, because many parents are very much concerned about pupil conduct and feel they can contribute to the identification of solutions.

One school used this approach to resolve lunchroom conduct problems. Parents were asked to assist lay hostesses during the lunch periods. As a result of their experience, these parents saw, first-hand, what the problems were, spent a considerable amount of time discussing the problems with other parents, and provided enough community support to help the school accomplish the following results:

1. More parents became concerned about how their own children were behaving.
2. Another lunchroom supervisor was hired.
3. Parents volunteered to serve as substitutes whenever a lunchroom supervisor was ill, or for other reasons was absent on a given day.

The scheduling of coffees in various parents' homes can be a continuous method of building positive community pressure points. This method can be done in several different ways.

1. The school administrators and one or two other staff members can attend a coffee with the idea in mind of discussing problems peculiar to that particular area and enlisting active parental support in solving these problems. This approach can be effective in dealing with such localized situations as student fights at bus stops, student loitering on lawns, and pupil conduct on buses.
2. Teachers of the same grade level can invite parents to an informal coffee at the school to discuss problems peculiar to students in this grade level, discuss possible solutions, and define teacher and parent roles in eliminating the problems. The authors have found this method helpful in dealing with such concerns as class party activities, boy-girl relationships, student dress habits, and student-parent relationships focusing on pre and early adolescent development.

3. The school staff can use scheduled coffees in homes to obtain feedback, on small group informal basis, pertaining to localized parental concerns about the school operation, aspects parents like and suggestions they may have. When meetings such as these have been held in all neighborhoods of the school attendance area, the faculty can identify specific topics of concern and where these are. The staff can then concentrate, with parental involvement, on resolving the expressed concerns.

A positive result here is the parents' feeling the school administration and staff are sincerely interested in specific problems identified in every area. This helps change many parents' feelings that the school personnel don't listen or react more to what people say in another area. This "personalized attention" given to parents is just as important as individualizing learning demands for each child.

8

Solving Behavior Problems
Outside the Classroom

HOW TO: DEVELOP RULES FOR LUNCHROOM CONDUCT

One of the greatest challenges which the modern-day school must contend with is the school district lunch program. Many young people seem to think that the basic philosophy behind the program is one of picnic orientation, and that all of the home training relative to table manners is to be forgotten. At the opposite extreme is the need for good self-discipline on the part of all students so that the program will operate in an efficient, healthful manner. When one considers the number of varying backgrounds and customs that are brought together in a meal setting, plus the factors of age and immaturity, it is easy to understand why we have difficulties administering such a program. Even though many educators feel that schools should not have to accept the responsibility for such a program, the trend has been to expand the program to all levels of general education. In fact, it has become a major business concern within the school economic structure requiring the services of many specialized personnel.

It is not unusual to try to serve 500 students in a period of from 40 to 60 minutes. Special personnel, who usually have no training in working with students, must in unusually hurried periods of time accommodate the total school population. These two factors alone create problems which normal homes, restaurants, and or cafeterias never have to face. In order to operate a successful lunch program, one must consider:

1. The personalities of the people connected with the program and their training in working with students.
2. The adequacy of the facilities and their physical arrangement, which must be conducive to efficiency and cleanliness.
3. An appropriate time block which will allow students to buy and then eat their lunch without being hurried.
4. The decor of the cafeteria so that it creates a pleasant eating environment.
5. Appropriately displayed rules which will govern the operation of the cafeteria.
6. Published types of discipline punishment which will be used if rules and regulations are not adhered to. Following are a few of the basic types of punishment which might be used: (a) disciplinary work assignments within the lunch program such as helping to clean tables, being in charge of the stacking of dirty trays, taking the garbage cans out when they are full, picking up food items which are on the floor, cleaning walls, windows, etc., (b) assigned seating for a definite period of time, (c) taking a student out of the program for a specific period of time and making him bring a lunch from home, (d) indefinite suspension from participating in the hot lunch program, (e) requested parent observation of student behavior, (f) the requirement that if a student is removed from the program, parents must pick him up and take him home for lunch and bring him back at the end of the lunch period.
7. Maintenance of an up-to-date log of conduct of grade levels as well as students, and as incidents occur following of a progressive type of discipline programming. (*Example:* If a specific class has been giving troubles, indicate that after receiving their food and taking a seat that no one is allowed to leave those seats until everyone at the table is finished. When they are finished they will, as a group, be allowed then to return their trays to the appropriate area and then possibly go outside for a short period of time.)

HOW TO HANDLE: RESTROOM PROBLEMS

Unlike some European schools which have full-time adult restroom monitors, the American public schools must assign teachers to periodic supervisory responsibilities for such areas. Restrooms are difficult to supervise for obvious reasons. However, there is growing concern about the physical damage which is seemingly increasing in such areas. If the building has many lavatories, the school administration can select a few centrally located lavatories which can be easily supervised for use, and close the rest to student use. If the building uses a pass system (sign out–check in), potential problem children can be quickly identified and supervised more closely with respect to lavatory problems.

Students will also respond positively to restroom care if they have some type of input into the general maintenance of the area. One school that was having problems elected to encourage the art department to adopt the area as a special art project. Bathroom doors became special challenges as they attempted to turn them into pieces of worthy art. One such door won a special art prize for its uniqueness of color and design in an art show. Walls were painted and cleanliness was stressed. The students began to take care of the area just because they had invested so much of their personal time in trying to correct a problem.

Restroom facilities are closely associated with sex. For this reason many unique problems come to the surface, which in turn makes the need for careful supervision mandatory especially for health reasons. It is very important that students who, in a physical sense, cannot handle the responsibility of the restroom be identified, and that parents be informed of their behavior.

One type of discipline for restroom offenders is the assigned maintenance of the area during the day and after school.

HOW TO: SET RULES FOR CLASS PASSING TIMES

There is no supervision like consistent adult supervision. All faculty members must assume their share of such responsibilities. As classes pass from one period to another, all staff members should assist in hall, stairs, and classroom supervision. It is not enough to simply request that staff members accept this chore, for this responsibility, like classroom discipline, sets the pattern for the following class as well as the overall program. The middle level student is not very safety oriented, and therefore the teacher has a responsibility to instruct in this area as well as the academics.

Some schools have been forced to rely upon parent volunteers to help as hall monitors. Large city schools have hired full-time policemen to be in charge of these responsibilities. Whoever we use, the fact remains that it is an area of deep concern and special need.

Using student monitors has not proven to be very successful unless older, more mature students will accept such assignments. One school pays students to accept this responsibility, and they have found that their problems in this area have decreased immeasurably.

School administrators should be aware of the need for careful planning with respect to student supervision in the building of new facilities. Design is nice, but not when it becomes more important than how a building should function.

Student leaders should be consulted about special problems in this area and asked for suggestions on how to solve such problems. A few such leaders have offered the following suggestions: (1) staggered class passing times; (2) having older students start their programs early and get out early; (3) assigning interested students to such responsibilities and giving them a free lunch in return for their services.

HOW TO: PREVENT GRAFFITI

Attempting to solve the problem of graffiti is a never-ending one. Such a problem seems to occur in streaks and, interestingly enough, takes on many forms relative to written expression. Over the years the authors have found that the following techniques help solve the problem.

1. Via your regular maintenance program, try to keep walls, desks, and rooms clean.
2. Assign students who are guilty of this offense after-school work detention to clean up the mess and the classroom in general.
3. Have a student bulletin board whereby messages might be posted in a positive way. Make sure that the bulletin board area is large enough for such items as posters. Have a student

council committee be in charge of the board and be responsible for making sure that it is not abused. Rules which govern the board should be made with students involved. Such rules should then be posted in an appropriate place so that all can see. School personnel should periodically check the board to make sure that it is functioning properly. Encourage good art students to help decorate the board and keep it attractive.

4. Keep in mind that much graffiti is done with no maliciousness in mind. Be fair but firm in assigning discipline. (Doodling and graffiti are not far apart in practice, even though in principle they serve differing purposes.)

HOW TO: ASSIST STUDENTS THROUGH THE PROBLEM OF FELT NEED TO PROVE ADULTHOOD

Many middle level students have a need to prove or show off their growth as they mature. When done in a proper manner and with discreteness, this display is a beautiful process. However, when it is done with a desire for exhibitionism, it can be extremely distasteful. This need can take many forms such as: (1) bullying, (2) provocative dress, (3) abusive or vulgar languages, (4) amateurish display of adult habits such as smoking, drinking alcoholic beverages, etc., and (5) overt interest in the opposite sex to the point of being obnoxious or abusive (fondling, vulgarity, etc.).

Such acting out, when not carried to extremes, is all a part of the adolescents' growth patterns. When it is carried to extremes, immediate counseling is necessary. Parents and school personnel must work cooperatively to bring about a common sense factor, and should consider the following techniques:

1. Developing and having in the curriculum program special courses which allow for the study of human growth both from a physical as well as mental viewpoint.
2. Use of group counseling to show that to a degree such behavior is normal and to try to establish limits as to what is normal and what is extreme.
3. Use of a positive approach when such behavior is observed, explaining to the student that you can understand his urges but that extremism destroys the beauty of such growth

patterns, and that more self-control is needed. The teacher might also indicate that there is a proper time and place for everything including the student's behavior.

Middle level students often attempt to prove their growth toward adulthood by showing aggressive independence in decision-making. Student efforts here are revealed in such social areas as selecting friends, dating, keeping late hours, expecting teachers to "not treat us as children," and reacting to staff members in the same manner teachers react to them. This is all a part of the maturation process. As such, the teacher should attempt to deal with inadequate student attempts in decision-making in a positive manner, even though the teacher's actions are corrective in nature. Positive corrective actions the teacher can take include the following:

1. Have students identify traits they want in each friend and how these traits can benefit them. Each student, then, is encouraged to privately analyze his own social groups in terms of these traits in order to help him assess the influence of the group on his actions.
2. Have students develop a social code of conduct—recommended guidelines of action for the student body that take into consideration student, staff, and parent thinking concerning school social activities. This encourages students and adults to work together in focusing on student concerns.
3. Develop a class profile, a simple listing of social and maturation characteristics of each class. This can serve as an effective method for helping you decide the actions you can take to best interact with students. The profile should be updated every nine weeks.

HOW TO HANDLE: GANG FIGHTS

Due to the apparent danger which could be the result of gang fights, educators try to do their best to see that they do not occur. Due to the fact that we are in a unique position to observe the development of gangs, we have a unique responsibility of seeing that parents know what is taking place and what the consequences might be. This is probably the best way of keeping gang action at a minimum, whether its direction is oriented toward groups with the school or toward groups from other schools.

Leaders of gangs should be counseled as to the responsibility that goes with their positions. The members of the gang should also be approached about their actions and the possible consequences.

If gangs seem to want to ignore the warnings of parents and educators, school administrators will want to call in civil authorities to council about the law, malicious assault, etcetera.

All educators should heed the warnings about prospective gang action, and inform proper authorities at the earliest moment possible. There is an old saying, "Let them fight, they might knock some sense into their heads!" It is true that that might be the only way they will learn; however, if the information is available and someone does get hurt, we have not accepted our responsibility as educators.

All of the preceding thoughts should be considered when dealing with gangs. Hopefully such negative actions can be reoriented into something positive.

Some specific actions teachers can take to help avoid gang fights are:

1. Have the leaders of each group meet with selected staff members to discuss reasons for group conflicts, how these problems can be resolved, and the responsibilities members of each group will assume to insure that fighting will not recur.
2. Invite a staff member from the emergency room of a local hospital to describe his experiences in dealing with injuries resulting from gang fights.
3. Provide the involved middle level students the opportunity to discuss with responsible high-school students how older students resolve group conflicts without resorting to violence. Emphasis here should be on how the younger students view their own participation in the high-school activities.
4. Identify the social strengths of each group and request assistance from each group for help in accomplishing tasks around the school. Parents can also be encouraged to ask each group for help in solving local community problems, such as helping install needed park playground equipment, helping identify solutions to neighborhood problems, provid-

ing opportunities for members of various neighborhood student groups to serve on a community-school youth council, and developing programs whereby physical energy can be expended in a sports program which has as its goal good sportsmanship.

HOW TO: STOP THE PRACTICE OF HAZING

Hazing, at first glance, seems to be an innocent way of initiating younger students into the higher grades. Many middle level students, however, do not have the maturity to know when to quit relative to this kind of involvement with younger students. As has been proven many times, this kind of action on the part of students can easily wind up with assault charges being filed, followed up by court action. Angry parents have a difficult time trying to figure out why their young people should get involved with older students in this way.

What most people forget is the resultant fear that such incidents can create, a fear that can easily scar a young person for life. There is a great deal of difference between being put upon or hazed by someone you know as versus a total stranger, who is possibly more abusive than a friend.

Student and parent bulletins should discourage such a practice. The basic rules which govern the school should include the fact that the practice is not wanted and will not be tolerated. Offenders should be dealt with in a very firm manner. If this sort of practice occurs on the last day of school, report cards should be held and parents and student should be required to come in together, so that the rule can be discussed and the reasons for such a rule enumerated.

HOW TO: PREVENT THE SELLING
OF CANDY AND OTHER ITEMS TO STUDENTS

The majority of school rules are very clear about prohibiting students from selling items such as candy, gum, and drinks to other students. In a day and age when drugs of all sorts are readily available to the teen world, it becomes imperative that this rule be enforced and that parents and students understand the reasons for such a rule.

Parents should be immediately notified of such actions by their children, and all materials confiscated and destroyed. Offenders should be counseled and an initial punishment exacted. If the offender continues to try to sell such items, suspension with the possibility of expulsion should be considered. Too many students will accept anything from anyone at anytime in complete confidence, even though they do not know the giver. The tragedies resulting from such naiveté are numerous and uncalled for. The training to resist such a temptation starts in the home and must be continued within the schools. There are some students who, because of their insecurity, will try anything on a dare. Teachers can easily identify the latter type of student and work with his needs. However, the former type of student could be any student at any time under any circumstance, and it is with this student that a general educational program about such a problem will normally succeed if the teaching is done early enough in the child's life.

HOW TO HANDLE:
ADMINISTRATIVE SEARCHES OR SHAKEDOWNS

The term shakedown, as used by the authors, has a double meaning. When students attempt to extort money from other members of the student body, we use it in referring to the extortion attempt that takes place. On the other hand, when it is used in relationship to administrator action it refers to the act of searching a student's person in order to try to locate stolen or illegal items which might be on that person's being. By the time students reach the middle school level, offenders who would be capable of and willing to create a situation in which students' lockers and their personal beings must be checked are pretty hardened characters. This type of student would willingly allow his peers as well as himself to be placed in the embarrassing situation which would result in an administrative search or shakedown. Because he would allow others to go through such a negative personal experience and never admit their guilt or their involvement (even though he knows that peers know who committed such acts), he forces teachers and administrators to seek out missing or illegal items. In doing so, school personnel must be careful and stay within the law. Two things must be thought about prior to using the search-shakedown technique: (1) Federal and state laws, and (2) the element of timeliness. Most states give school administrators the right to search, but not to the extent of overt personal offense.

If the cause for considering a shakedown has occurred within the last few minutes, there will be some probability of success; however, if some time has lapsed or if the teacher in charge cannot place a time element on the act that has created the problem, it is best not to use this technique. One might also give consideration to the make-up of the class. If there are many students in the class who have a past history of such a problem, the fact that they are experienced in such matters gives them an edge in not being caught.

The author does not feel that shakedowns accomplish much except the creation of a great deal of animosity. It would be better to see if members of the class can handle the situation among themselves. One teacher who found herself in such a predicament told the class that she was going to leave them alone for a few minutes and that when she returned to the class, she wanted to see an item which had been stolen from a student on her desk. After approximately five minutes she returned to the class to find the article on her desk. She praised the class for handling the matter and talked briefly about the problem of theft. Students, at a later time, thanked her for handling the matter in that manner. She was asked what she would have done if the item had not been returned, and she indicated that she would have probably used the technique of a shakedown. Her experience with middle level students had taught her to reach in a positive manner to solve such problems, and not to create embarrassment for the majority who are innocent. She did indicate that at a later date students told her who had committed the act, and that they only confirmed her suspicions.

HOW TO: PREVENT PROBLEMS SUCH AS ERASER AND CHALK FIGHTS

Eraser and chalk fights usually occur at the beginning or ending of a class, when supervision is in a state of flux or when a teacher leaves the classroom and the room is left totally unsupervised. It takes a great deal of thought and group counseling to prepare a class for the responsibility of being left on its own. Peer pressure is the key which keeps students under control at times when teachers are faced with multi-responsibilities. It is not an accident that some teachers can leave a class on it's own and never have problems. The class, as has been indicated in prior sections, must be involved in the establishment of the rules which govern it. They must be taught to feel that to a considerable degree they are in charge of their own destiny. The few who are not capable of managing such on their own will be brought into line by the majority. If a teacher wishes to establish this kind of rapport with a class, he must, on purpose, periodically leave the class on it's own for short periods of time. The teacher might also in the beginning tell the class that he is leaving and where he is going. This alerts the more responsible students to reach for leadership roles. Later on the teacher will find that he does not need to inform the class of his leaving.

Some teachers solve the problem of eraser and chalk fights by removing the articles from the chalk trays and storing them in an area that can be secured. When such articles are needed, students then know where to go get them. Assigning students this kind of responsibility will keep down confusion and make for an orderly procedure. A teacher might also have offenders stand at the classroom door until personally allowed to enter the classroom. Such students might also be refused privileges that the majority of students receive, such as going to the restroom without supervision and leaving their desks without permission.

One teacher who, when her back was turned, was bothered by students throwing objects such as chalk and pencils finally decided that group punishment was the only answer. She talked with the class about the problem and informed them that if such an incident happened again, she would keep the entire class after school for a detention block of time. The students challenged her threat of discipline. The teacher was one step ahead of them, however, for she had mailed a statement of the problem to the home of each parent and asked for their support in solving her dilemma. The parents responded in a positive manner and the throwing of any type of article ended. Her forethought in the solving of the problem was the key to it's success.

When a student is caught doing such an act, and if the class had been warned about such behavior, a teacher might assign that student to the responsibility of taking care of the erasers and chalk for the remainder of the term, including daily cleaning of the erasers immediately after school or during lunch break. At first the task may seem fun to the student, but after a short period of time it will become a chore.

HOW TO: PREVENT RUNNING
AND PUSHING IN THE HALLS

The answer to solving the problem of horseplay in the halls is one of adequate supervision, which is discussed earlier in this chapter. However, there are times when the halls are not adequately supervised, especially when classes are in session, and it is during this time that school personnel will have to reach for other techniques to control them. The following suggestions might be considered:

1. Assign one of the staff members who is involved in planning to periodically check the halls.
2. Have custodians periodically sweep the halls during the time when classes are in session, and ask them to help in a temporary supervisory capacity.
3. If the building schedule accommodates study halls, assign older, more reliable students to a type of hall responsibility.
4. Place the desks of parent volunteers who work with the faculty so that they can help supervise the halls.
5. Placement of specialized personnel offices (administrative, counseling, etc.) so that doors and windows give eye control over the halls.
6. Use of a pass system whereby students are checked for a pass each time they are met in the hall. This means that a student has been given permission by a teacher to be in the halls at a specific time. (The pass indicates the time the student left a specific area, where he is going, and the person or area receiving him indicates what time the student arrived and also the time he left to return.) Such passes should be collected, held, and not destroyed for a period of 48 hours.

While the new open concept schools do away with halls per se, their large open-space areas still require constant supervision. Team planning areas should be built to accommodate such a need.

HOW TO: CONTROL WATER GUNS, BALLOONS, AND SQUIRT BOTTLES

At various times during the academic year, water guns, balloons, squirt bottles, and other such items become a fad. The majority of such items are harmless, but they do upset a program. Their restriction should initially be limited by being a part of the school rules which students and parents receive at the beginning of the school year. The rule should indicate that such items, when found, will be immediately confiscated and not returned.

Schools use many techniques to try to keep such items from becoming a problem. A few suggestions are:

1. Since the prohibiting of such items is a part of the rules, immediately bring students found using such to the administrative office for discipline. If a class has been disrupted by their actions, after-school work sessions should be assigned and their admittance to the class which was disrupted be refused for a specific period of time.
2. Require the guilty student to call and ask his parents to come and pick up the item he used to disrupt the class before he can be readmitted to class.
3. Quietly confiscate the item which is being used to disrupt the class and say nothing. This often defeats the student's desire for attention.

HOW TO: SOLVE STUDENT LOCKER PROBLEMS

As necessary as lockers are to students, they can be a never-ending problem to school officials. Many students consider lockers a type of play-share item, when in fact they should be looked upon as a privacy-storage area. The fact that lockers are a necessary part of school equipment means that the rules and regulations governing them must be clear and fully understood.

Teachers who have responsibility for specific lockers should discuss locker problems with the students, making sure that students understand why lockers can be a problem, and how to avoid the problems. Following are a few suggestions:

1. Assign lockers to students in such a manner that teachers who have responsibility for periodic inspections will cover lockers which are close to their classroom door. The teacher will then know the students who are in charge of those lockers, and will be able to supervise the conduct around them more closely.
2. Assign problem students to areas near offices where lockers are more closely supervised.
3. Deny consistent offenders any locker use for a given period of time, with two days being the minimum penalty time. The inconvenience of carrying all his property around will definitely help a student to recognize the value of locker convenience.
4. Since hall control and locker control are synonymous, warn students found loitering in the halls, especially around their locker area, about being tardy and send them immediately to their class. If the problem continues, the student or students should be sent to the appropriate administrator for disciplinary action.
5. Periodically check lockers for neatness and cleanliness. When a poor housekeeper has been found, make sure that he understands what standards you wish the class to maintain. If the problem continues, have the student meet you after school on special days to see that this is accomplished. Surprise inspections help students develop a habit of cleanliness, especially if there is a penalty attached for those who are untidy. Lockers can also serve as a picking up point for various commodities not wanted in or around a school. Items such as alcoholic beverages, cigarettes, drugs, pornography, and even candy can create real problems for students and school personnel. Lockers of students who are more prone to try to bring such items on board should be checked regularly.
6. Do not assign close friends as locker partners, if it is imperative to have more than one student to a locker.

7. Assign locker areas by age groups. This reduces problems between younger and older students.
8. If necessary to reduce student loitering, shorten passing times.

HOW TO: SOLVE THE PROBLEM OF CRASHING SCHOOL EVENTS

A few years back the answer to solving the problem of outside students crashing school events amounted to nothing more than having adequate supervision available. In this day and age the trend has been to hire professional personnel to work in conjunction with school staff. Off-duty policemen and/or trained private personnel seem to solve the personnel needs for schools.

If warnings about such impending problems are given, school authorities might want to consider the following techniques:

1. If a specific school is involved, a telephone call to the proper leadership will probably head off any negative student involvement.
2. Do not hesitate to use or hire the services of police-trained personnel. Their attendance, in uniform, will probably be all that is needed.
3. Holding school events at the school and not in rented facilities permits a greater degree of crowd control.
4. If crashing is a possibility, it is important that the group having the party understand that that possibility exists and that some control over the door (entering and leaving practice) be exercised.

The problem of gate crashers might originate within your own building. If there are students involved in attempting to create such a problem, make sure that these students know that you are aware of it, and that if it happens you will hold them responsible for such an incident. Parents should be notified that their child is or could be involved in such a problem, and if it takes place what the consequences might be.

HOW TO: PREVENT RUDENESS TO VISITORS

Although rudeness to visitors is seldom a problem, it cannot be overlooked because of the impression it makes on the public.

There are many kinds of visitors who will come to a school: (1) parents, (2) guests, (3) professional associates, (4) substitute teachers, (5) student visitors, and so on. If rudeness is a problem to any one of these types of people, teachers and school authorities should take immediate steps to correct the matter. Offenders, with parents in attendance, should be counseled about manners and what manners mean to the public in general. Such counseling might provide a student's first look at what the public views as acceptable standards of conduct. We should remember that we are not just teachers of fact or subject matter, but that we are, in many cases, the only people who will have an opportunity to help mold a person into a successful adult. When rudeness toward peers, visitors, family, or friends is displayed, take a moment to discuss what it means in terms of a young person's future. This is a teachable moment that many teachers overlook.

There should be a written code of conduct for students to follow. This code should be discussed thoroughly at the beginning of the school year, and as incidents occur it should be brought up and discussed again and again.

9

Dealing with
Student Group Problems

HOW TO HANDLE: CLASSROOM LEADERSHIP
AND POWER STRUCTURE

Each class is a world unto itself. Because of the many personalities which are a part of the class structure, a teacher must play a coordinating role so that a balance takes place which will allow for the best educational environment possible.

As a class meets, it is not long before there is an emergence of individual and group leadership. It therefore becomes the responsibility of the teacher to either discourage or encourage the roles that each group or person will play.

If a negative group begins to assume leadership, the teacher will want to build its overall effectiveness and try to redirect the group's purpose.

1. A reclarification of the purposes of the class will be imperative. If the negative group will not allow this to take place, the leaders might have to be removed from the class permanently.
2. There should never be any doubt about the teacher's role in the class. If students challenge that role and try to overrule the teacher, it will be necessary to privately counsel the student leadership. If they are not receptive to allowing the class to progress, they must be dealt with in a very directive disciplinary way. Those students who respond in a positive

manner should be allowed to work within the class; those who balk should be reassigned to classes where negative leadership would not be accepted.

It is fascinating to watch how general leadership and a power structure evolve. Much of what takes place can be of a positive nature. Students tend to not want to waste their time. A teacher might capitalize on this fact and when an element of negative leadership appears, stop the progress of the class and indicate that nothing will continue until all are giving their attention to the class and the subject at hand.

It should be noted that even when a class is working well and the general leadership is positive and supportive, things might go wrong depending upon the interaction of all members of the class. If a point of unfairness seems to work its way into how subject matter is assigned or evaluated, the teacher must prepare to head off the flak created by normally supportive students—think through your reasons for doing such, and take an amount of time to explain why you are doing what you are doing. Do not be afraid to be honest in your deliberations for, in fact, by doing so the value of honesty is given its proper place.

Periodically you will want to allow student leadership to assume maximal roles of responsibility. This is done by slowly encouraging job responsibility. Allow students to periodically assume the teacher role. This can be done in many ways such as: (1) giving reports, (2) handing out or collecting assignments, (3) assignment as group leader for research or discussion projects, and (4) preparation and presentation of audiovisual material.

HOW TO: CONTROL TEACHER-STUDENT FUNCTIONING CLASHES

Is there a specific functioning role that teachers and/or students must follow? In a day and age when teachers try many techniques to help young people learn more effectively, functions must change in order to allow for varying degrees of maturity and ability. In the old days education followed a lecture-listen technique. Today it is not unusual for students, in the daily routine, to assume teacher responsibilities. The days of lecture-listen techniques have been changed to accommodate a third element called challenge. Students are encouraged to ask questions and also answer questions related to personal research and practical understanding.

Education therefore takes on an individualized approach and teachers must adapt to the fact that their role will be challenged and that this challenge, when done positively, is healthy.

Teachers must also become cognizant of the fact that each student will function differently depending upon background, experience, and ability. Each brings to the class a different set of values, mores, and folkways. This means that the teacher will have a greater challenge in making sure that all members of the class are accommodated in an educational sense. If there is a bit of wisdom to be shared it might be related to the fact that one should listen, observe, and then share his knowledge and experience as best he can. Students, in many ways, will relate to you their special needs, and if you are listening you will be able to help them.

HOW TO HANDLE: STUDENT RESENTMENT OF "PUT DOWN"

It is not unusual for a young student to become overbearing or abusive in his actions. If he does this in a positive display of exuberance, it will be received positively even though one might ask him to keep things under control. However, to the contrary, a negative interaction which disrupts the class will result in a "put down" that to a degree is aimed at placing a student in an embarrassing situation, hopefully to make him think twice before misbehaving again. One cannot predict how such a "put down" will be received. Examples of conduct that might result in a "put down" are: (1) a loud burp, (2) an uncouth remark, (3) speaking out without permission, (4) bothering other students, and (5) being out of one's seat without permission.

Typical examples of a "put down" would be: (1) ignoring the student, (2) making fun of the student in a derogatory manner, (3) cuffing the student on the hand or head, (4) making the student sit or stand in a special area, (5) using a special look to show your displeasure, (6) kidding the student about the problem when one is not really kidding, (7) making an offhand remark.

Each of the preceding examples can be used to put a student "in his place" for having upset class routine. However, many teachers are not aware of the methods they use because they are so much a part of their teaching routine. Put downs can be an effective teaching technique but they should be used with care and purpose. If you are in doubt about the techniques you use, ask your class for aid and I am sure that they will be more than honest.

Teachers should also remember that different techniques work on different students. If your "bag of tricks" is limited, you will periodically be in trouble, for if you use similar techniques with different students, some will be upset because they do not like to be compared to others and they will rate the degree or type of offense in terms of punishment. If they think you have been unfair they will tell you so!

HOW TO REACT TO: SPECIFIC STUDENT DEMANDS

How does a teacher or school administrator react when students make demands? Each person will react according to his background and experience, and depending upon how the request is made. These three factors play major roles in how schools are run.

Students who are in positions of responsibility should be counseled in the art of making friends and influencing people, for there is no better way to achieve success than to use a system based upon politeness and consideration.

Many teachers would be disappointed if students, as they grow and mature, did not make demands concerning class routine, study habits, and grades. The majority of middle level students know how to ask for special considerations. The few who have not developed appropriate techniques find themselves in a dilemma, for they usually make a big show with their request, only to have it turned down in a rather negative manner.

Teachers, when approached by students making demands, should:

1. Listen to the request and respond in a polite way.
2. If the request seems absurd, give an immediate answer with a brief statement of why. This is better than to keep the group in suspense.
3. If the request has been made in an impolite manner, take the time to explain your thoughts concerning the presentation and why you would probably react in a negative way.
4. Do not be afraid to be honest in explaining your thoughts concerning a demand. Young people will learn more when this occurs than if one tends to play politics with them.

5. If the request seems to be made honestly and is fair, even though one might not be able to respond positively because of rules, etc., tell the students your thoughts and if necessary give them direction.
6. Never respond to a demand with a negative answer such as "No, just because I have said no." This creates resentment which in time causes other problems.
7. If a student has been obnoxious and abusive in making a legitimate request, tell him no and explain to him that the answer will continue to be no until his manners improve.
8. Evaluate carefully the needs of the student body in terms of social interaction. If your student body has a failing in this respect, ask teachers (home economics and social studies) to add to the curriculum a section dealing with communication and manners.

HOW TO AVOID: THE "PARENT" APPROACH IN THE CLASSROOM

It is almost impossible for teachers who are parents not to assume a parental approach with their students, especially at the elementary and middle school level. It seems that we must preach in order to make sure that we have communicated in a thorough manner. The fact that we may state the problem and probable solution many times turns many students off, since it tells them that we do not consider them adult enough to get it the first time around. It takes a considerable amount of time to prepare a class for accepting adult-type routines, and yet it is important that we do this.

Teachers must use many techniques in trying to stay away from sounding like parents. They might:

1. With the aid of students, establish classroom rules which accept young people as young adults, assuming that they can and will accept the responsibilities that have been agreed upon.
2. Make sure that a student knows you are disappointed at his inability to accept responsibility, but do not make a big issue out of it.
3. If one must preach, tell students that you are preaching and tell them why! You might go so far as to indicate that you

will continue to preach until they accept and carry out responsibilities which all have agreed upon.

4. If the majority of the class is doing well and just a couple are having a rough time, take the couple aside and counsel them about their problems. Do not make the whole class have to listen to your lecture.

5. For a period of time you might want to do more preaching than teaching. Remember, however, that it is an easy way to turn off students.

6. Try not to get involved in a student's personal problems (for example: dress, cleanliness, grooming) during a class period. Ask him to see you at a later time. Approach him as an adult, teacher, and friend (not in reverse order) and be honest but gentle.

7. Some counselors make good teachers, but not all teachers make good counselors. Keep this in mind when approaching students in a parent-like manner. Do not feel offended if they ignore you, the fact is that you tried to help solve a problem. If this happens consistently, you might wish to reach for the help of special people like counselors if such a need arises again.

8. If a class or a student has a special problem, before you act in an attempt to solve the problem, share your concern with other members of the faculty. It is usually surprising how solutions will come to mind after such consultations.

One teacher uses the parental approach in a positive way. He has several hats that depict various personages. When he feels that he must drive a special point home, he peeks out and wears the appropriate hat. His parent hat looks like a 1920 gangster evening hat as worn by Chicago hoods. The students have responded very favorably to his approach, and have shown no resentment to being "preached at."

HOW TO: DEVELOP EFFECTIVE PLANS
FOR SUBSTITUTE TEACHERS

Middle level students often view the substitute teacher as an opportunity for challenge, even though with the regular teachers they are well-behaved and function in a business-like manner. Generally, this challenge of a substitute is a result of the regular teacher's not making clear to his students exactly what he expects of them in his absence in relation to behavior and learning performance. He assumes this emphasis will carry over during his absences. His students, however, often do not share this assumption.

Because of the pre and early adolescents' tendencies toward unexpected behavior, it is essential that the teacher plan carefully for class activities to be carried on during his absence. He must also plan follow-up actions in case students do not perform as expected during his absence or the substitute teacher did not function as expected. Preparing for a substitute teacher involves planning for both teacher and students in terms of behavior.

Though, practically speaking, the regular staff member has limited control over how a substitute performs, the teacher can delineate an action pattern that is consistent with what the students have learned to expect. The regular staff member can do this by developing a substitute folder that includes such pertinent information as:

1. Specific instructional methods to use.
2. Seating chart.
3. Names of student leaders.
4. Directions for homework, for testing, for collection and disposition of collected papers.
5. Class behavioral expectations.
6. Directions for care of room, supplies, and equipment.

After the teacher has developed the basic operational plans for the substitute teacher, he must then concern himself with clarifying his demands and expectations to his students. In addition to his making clear to the class that the normal classroom procedures are to be followed, the teacher must impress on the students that:

1. The substitute teacher is carrying out his directions.
2. The teacher will follow up on any rule infractions.
3. The students have certain responsibilities to:
   a) Help the substitute work toward specified learning objectives.
   b) Maintain a positive student reputation.

4. The substitute is, for the time he is in the class, a member of the faculty.
5. The regular teacher will hold students responsible for their actions.
6. Good student response is positive public relations because substitute teachers do talk about their experiences.

A key action of the regular teacher, of course, is the manner and consistency in which he follows up on any negative incidents occurring in the class during the time the substitute is in charge. Informing a class about follow-up actions commits the teacher to carrying out these actions. Consequently, he must commit himself only to those actions he knows he can enforce. These must be practical and behavior-oriented.

Various actions the teacher can use are:

1. Inform counselors and appropriate administrators of what he expects of the students and the substitute; follow-up actions he will take in case of serious misbehavior.
2. In individual cases of misbehavior, meet with violators and their parents, explaining what happened and ways the parents can help to insure the actions will not recur.
3. Make arrangements for chronic violators to be moved out of the classroom when subsequent substitute teachers are needed.
4. Provide opportunities for the offending student to recreate his actions and have the class react to them. Under different conditions, the offensive behavior is seen in a different light.
5 Have the class critique their own actions during the time the substitute was present and develop remedial action pertaining to overall class behavior.

Since no two people function in the same manner, it behooves the teacher to develop instructional procedures that are relatively universal in nature; that is, to provide activities and method suggestions that most substitutes can follow. Providing activities and suggestions that less experienced and less effective persons can handle helps insure a greater possibility of success for the substitute.

Not all districts give individual teachers the opportunity to request specific substitutes. However, where this is possible, each teacher should keep an updated assessment chart of his substitutes. In this way he can:

1. Request substitutes that have proved themselves capable;
2. Better plan for substitutes because he has in mind a better picture of how available substitutes function;
3. Develop a clearer picture of how his students behave when substitutes are in charge of his classes.

HOW TO AVOID: STUDENT CONFRONTATIONS

Confrontations between students and between student and teacher cannot always be avoided at the middle level because of the sudden arising of a particular situation and the unexpected reaction of a student within this situation. However, the teacher, through planning and directive action, can reduce confrontations to a minimum. He can do this first by identifying several concepts basic to the development of student-teacher conflicts. Among these are the following:

1. There are times when teacher conduct is the cause of conflict.
2. Many times confrontation is the culmination of an observable student action or reaction pattern.
3. Extent and severity of individual confrontations generally can be controlled by the teacher.
4. Confrontations often are the result of temporary flare-ups by middle level students.

Quite often a confrontation challenge is an isolated student action with a corresponding reaction by the teacher bringing about an actual confrontation situation. Unusual, suddenly agressive action by the teacher places the guilty student in a defensive position. He sees no way out of the predicament. His only thought then is to yield, and consequently lose face, or stand his ground, waiting to react to the teacher's next move. Here, the teacher controls the situation.

To control the extent and severity of a student-teacher confrontation, the teacher should:

1. Through observation and talk ascertain the emotional distress level of the student.
2. Speak quietly, firmly, and to the point.
3. Find out as quickly as possible the cause of the student's overreaction.
4. Identify student's objectives and any conflicts between these and teacher/class objectives.
5. Talk with student with other students around.
6. Deal with the future, not the past.

Perhaps the most effective method of avoiding student confrontations is to anticipate and plan for them before they happen. This involves the teacher's developing a record-keeping procedure that enables him to identify student conduct patterns and teacher action patterns. Figures 9-1 and 9-2 present two useful forms the teacher can use as part of his recording procedure.

PROBLEM ANALYSIS FORM

Student _Eric Boswell_   Date _October 7_

Class _8th Choir_

ACTIVITY Group singing in preparation for a school concert	STUDENT MISCONDUCT hitting other students, talking while other students were trying to sing their parts—lack of self-direction and assuming responsibility.
LEARNING OBJECTIVE(S) Development of pride in singing capabilities Development of self-discipline Showing respect for others	TEACHER ACTION AT TIME OF MISCONDUCT helping small groups practice their parts of the songs
TEACHER FOLLOW-UP OBSERVATION OF STUDENT ACTIONS Date _October 8 & 9_ CONDUCT IMPROVEMENT NOTED Student desire to be in program and parent pressure resolved problem	TEACHER REMEDIAL ACTION talked with student and parent—not serious—a first time action. Student informed would not be in program DATE PARENT NOTIFIED _10-7_

Figure 9-1

STUDENT BEHAVIOR PLANNING FORM

Student _Adam Wells_   Age _14_   Date _Sept. 7, 19–_

STUDENT STRENGTHS
Seeing strengths of others
Can follow directions
Pleasant; good sense of humor
Can adjust quickly to new situations

POTENTIAL IMPROVEMENT AREAS
Demanding less personal attention
Developing capability to see the effects of his actions on others
Becoming more confident in making his own decisions

STUDENT EMPHASIS ACTIVITIES
Serving as a group leader
Working on limited independent study activities
Developing personal conduct expectations

TEACHER SUPPORT ACTIVITIES
Scheduling regular student-teacher conferences
Provide opportunities for student to account for his own decisions
Show personal interest in student
Help student develop a self-appraisal technique

PROGRESS APPRAISAL   Date _Nov. 4, 19–_

During the past quarter, Adam has honestly tried to look at himself and his effect on others. He has become more confident in ability to do good work. However, he still tends to dominate group discussions. He and I plan to devote increased emphasis to this and to his learning to work more on his own without disturbing others.

Teacher _Miss Owen_

Copy to parent

Figure 9-2

The continuous use of a form (Figure 9-1) such as the Problem Analysis Form provides the student and teacher with a record of each incident and remedial action taken. The use of the form also helps the teacher, and any support people who may become involved, to recognize any type of negative student behavior pattern that may be developing. It also provides the teacher with a record of remedial actions taken and the extent of their effectiveness.

In working with the involved parent, the teacher also has a continuous record on file. This provides more supportive evidence for the teacher when there is parent-teacher disagreement. Also, it can help the parent in working with his child because he knows, on a continuing basis, what the child is doing, what the teacher is doing, and what he, the parent, must do if the problem is to be resolved.

The student, at any given time, is able to look at his pattern of actions in the classroom and to see the effects of his actions. This is particularly important to the middle level student because of his tendency to encompass an entire student body.

The record-keeping procedure is of little use, however, unless the teacher makes use of it in terms of individual student behavior patterns and purposes. Following is a case in point.

A seventh-grade student, during the first three months of his Spanish class, challenged the teacher: "Why am I in this class, anyway? I didn't ask to be put in here and I'm not going to take any more of your picking on me."

The teacher had been keeping a record of the student's behavior patterns. From this she summarized his major problems.

Student Behavior Level	Desired Behavior
1. Functions only with students he knows well	Adequate adjustment to different peer groups
2. Attempts to copy from other students	Develop confidence in own capability to do satisfactory work
3. Tends to bully small students	Respect individual student differences and feelings
4. Constant refusal to follow school rules	Recognition of need for rules and each student's following them; recognition of value of group functioning needs

As the teacher perused her record of the student's behavior and compared it with the identified desired behaviors, she began to see a performance pattern developing and identified specific conflict areas. She could readily see what class situations and teacher pressures could cause the student to demonstrate desirable behavior.

As a result of this planning and record keeping, the teacher was able to avoid most situations that could result in the boy's challenging her. Also, she was able to plan more effectively in terms of the child's needs as revealed by her conflict list. By changing procedures and teacher actions, she eventually was able to communicate with the boy to the extent that by the end of the semester, he was readily discussing his concerns and problems with the teacher. Student flare-ups still arose occasionally, but the boy recognized them as symptoms of his own frustration and no longer attempted personal challenges of the teacher.

HOW TO: REDUCE NEGATIVE TEACHER REACTIONS

Effective teaching is based on positive student-teacher interaction. This interaction is directly affected by the overt and subtle actions of both teacher and pupil. Most discipline situations stress the conduct of the student. However, in many cases, it is negative teacher action that either initiates or stimulates negative student reaction. Consequently, the teacher can help avoid, and eliminate, many student discipline problems by being observant of his own actions and how these stimulate student behavior. This observation also involves the teacher's being aware of the kinds and extents of his own inconsistencies.

The following incident illustrates this need:

Dennis was a thirteen-year-old boy who would eventually make his way in the world, but who had continuous difficulty functioning within the academic confines of the school. He was seemingly at odds with his teachers as a result of his inability to consider the effects of his actions. Along with this, Dennis was easily led by older students but was a leader among boys younger than he. He used younger students to do things he was afraid to do just as the older boys used him.

His counselors and all but one of his teachers were aware of this and attempted to work with him with this singular functioning pattern of his in mind. In most cases, they were able to gain positive responses from Dennis until he became involved with the older boys, again. The teachers, then, had to start their behavioral modification efforts over again. The important point with these teachers was that for a short time, at least, they would help Dennis reveal progress. Also, he would be able to relate his problems to future actions.

The one teacher had problems with Dennis every day, primarily because he expected Dennis to behave according to unchanging class rules that made no allowance for individual differences. Another major cause of the teacher-student functioning differences was the teacher's habit of relating his corrective endeavors only to things Dennis had done in the past. The boy had little opportunity and no encouragement to view his misconduct in terms of what was expected of him on an ongoing basis.

Dennis often stated to his counselor and the assistant principal that he didn't really know what the teacher wanted. All he knew was that the teacher "rode me all the time." Unfortunately, Dennis was correct. The teacher was continually nagging and finding fault with Dennis, rather than using an incident as a teaching-learning opportunity. Eventually Dennis came to dislike the teacher so much he made no effort to respond to the teacher.

The situation was resolved only by moving Dennis out of the teacher's class. This, however, did not help the teacher improve, nor did it erase the bitter memories related to one teacher and school in general from Dennis' mind.

The teacher can avoid negative reactions through such approaches as the following:

1. Study the students as they work on their assignments. Note individual student characteristics such as concentration spans, frustration levels, amount of aimless activity, handling of quiet class time. Awareness of these will give the teacher insight into how a student works. The teacher, while observing, can make mental notes as to how he should handle each potential problem.
2. Totem-pole the students according to how well they act in terms of classroom behavior expectations. This will help the teacher identify potential individual student trouble areas.
3. Consider your own teaching actions—how many of these are part of lesson planning, how many are simple reactions, how many can be classified as "parental" actions?
4. Identify student-teacher conflict incidents—were these resolved primarily for teacher satisfaction or for improvement of learner performance?

HOW TO: RESOLVE CLASSROOM ORGANIZATION
AND STUDENT MATURATION CONFLICTS

Middle level students are very changeable in growth characteristics, in outlooks, in interests, and in feelings. The effective teacher changes and adjusts his classroom structure and organization to parallel these student changes. This does not mean the teacher has to change the basic procedures of his classroom as much as he needs to change his own methods of functioning. However, the basic structure and demands must be flexible enough to permit changes in teacher and student behavior. This necessitates the teacher's identifying possible situations and how he will react to them.

Student Situation	*Teacher Reactions*
1. Student consistently failing to listen to directions	1. Notify him that he is to repeat the directions after the teacher has given them.
	2. Have him write the directions as they are given.
2. Students noisy and playing around when the teacher is not in the room	1. Make recording of class sounds while teacher is absent. Have class identify persons, purpose of comments made and what the teacher should expect from the class.
	2. Have an assignment folder up to date. Identify a reliable student to read the assignment.
3. Writing on desks	1. Have students provide themselves with scratch paper if they must "doodle" while listening. The paper is to be given to the teacher.
	2. Make these students official room caretakers who are responsible for desk cleanliness. Peer pressure helps discourage writing on desks.

An underlying purpose of these teacher actions is the development of clearly-defined patterns of conduct expected from the students. This pattern of conduct must be flexible enough to take into account student conduct ranging from thoughtlessness to deliberate actions.

As a rule of thumb, remedial demands in the classroom should involve some type of overt action from the offending students.

This serves two purposes—these students must do work under direct supervision for a clearly-identified purpose and the violators must do more than passively listen to the teacher's corrective lecture. The physical remedial action must be handled so that the students involved cannot be allowed to show off and so that they are held responsible for describing to the teacher why they deserved the punishment and what action the teacher should take the next time.

It cannot be overemphasized that though both the classroom structure and the teacher must be flexible enough to respond to student changes, the teacher must remain the authority in control. He accomplishes his purposes through fairness, consistency, and humanness. The teacher accomplishes this through immediacy of action and a minimum of talk. Too many discipline problems occur at the middle level because the teacher delayed actions. It doesn't take middle students long to identify a given teacher's "action point."

HOW TO: COORDINATE RULE DEMANDS
AND FUNCTIONING PATTERNS DESIRED BY STUDENTS

"Rules are made to be enforced; rules are made to be broken." Often these two opposing viewpoints are typical of the differences in behavioral outlooks by teachers and students. Staff members are expected to deal with these differences in an arbitrary manner; that is, the conduct rule comes first; the student and his performance patterns are secondary. It is only natural to expect a resulting conflict between students and teacher when this philosophy is present.

When conduct rules are implemented as behavioral guidelines and learning objectives, they become part of the overall curriculum and not, as many pupils view them, the personal concern of the teacher. It the teacher is to gain student support of classroom rules, he must give attention to:

1. Considering student backgrounds, values, and capabilities.
2. Determining what specific rules are needed beyond the normal functioning patterns of the student.
3. Encouraging students to participate in the identification of rule needs and the making of rules.
4. Clarifying student and teacher roles and responsibilities in implementing the rules.

Even though students help make rules, the teacher cannot expect that there will be no violations or conflicts. Consequently, he must plan accordingly. Following are some methods and techniques he can use to resolve conflicts resulting from differences between rule demands and desired student functioning patterns.

1. Periodically review the classroom rules with the students, reevaluating each one, changing it to fit the present class needs. Remember, the original rules were made in terms of a past status quo.
2. Be careful about adding many new rules. Ideally, the number of rules would be reduced as pupils learn to function in terms of group requirements.
3. Identify the rules most frequently violated. Discuss these with the class. Concentrate on the reduction of violations in these areas, setting these as objectives for both teacher and students.
4. The teacher must follow the rules himself.

Too often rules are unchanging while students are changing. This, together with the teacher's need to judge each violation as an individual matter, can lead to the teacher's being accused of unfairly enforcing classroom regulations. To help avoid this, the teacher can take such approaches as:

1. Explaining to students that each violation will be handled on an individual basis, and why.
2. Having students rank probable violations in order of seriousness and consequent equivalent remedial actions.
3. Providing each violator opportunity to explain to the class his actions, reasons for them, expected results from them, and how his actions were contrary to acceptable group behavior.
4. Being consistent in time as to the promptness that remedial action is taken in each case.
5. Discussing with the students, in a nonthreatening way, exactly what the teacher expects and why. Have the students write these things down and keep them in their notebooks for continuous reference.

A ninth-grade teacher found that using the procedures above avoided many student-teacher arguments based on such excuses as "I forgot," "you didn't give me another chance," and "others have done it and you didn't do anything to them." In following the procedures above, she did not have to rely on her memory as far as being consistent in following rules. She had developed a plan of action that all students knew would be followed.

The procedures saved her a great deal of trouble and time when she was assigned a group of students who had the habit of arguing with each other and with the teacher. When a teacher would attempt to correct a member of the class, other students would join in, trying to influence the teacher's decisions. However, when the teacher took time to explain the procedures that would be followed, when she stayed within the procedural framework and she proved she couldn't be swayed by vocal students, the class gradually accepted the outlined procedures. By the end of the first quarter, student misbehavior had diminished and pupils who were guilty of misconduct no longer received vocal support from their friends.

10

Utilizing a Discipline Ladder of Referral

Discipline procedures, for maximum effectiveness, need to be developed on a systematic basis. As in other instructional areas, student behavior development must be done in terms of individualization, specific objectives, progressive functioning demands, and applied performance. To maintain consistency in these areas, the school staff should utilize a ladder of referral structure. Through this approach, teachers can function more on a basis of coordinated behavioral expectations and be less subject to parent and student criticism related to retaliations, overreaction, and inconsistency.

HOW TO: DEVELOP THE LADDER OF REFERRAL

The development of the ladder of referral should involve representatives of those groups who will be directly affected by discipline rules and procedures—staff, parents, and students. Through this approach, the school staff gains feedback from parents and students relative to potential effectiveness of various disciplinary measures, parental support of, and desire for, particular disciplinary actions, and community expectations related to staff and student conduct. These expectations determine parent support and consequent teacher effectiveness.

Parent expectations vary from permissiveness to tight authoritarian control. Consequently, the staff must assume leadership in developing the referral guidelines within which they, parents, and students can function. This leadership will help insure that the discipline policies, practices and referral structure are consistent with the other instructional/learning phases of the school.

This type and structure of a ladder of referral will vary according to the operational framework and demands of each school and according to the value structure of the school staff and community. There are, however, some basic aspects that are common to effective referral practices. Among these are:

1. Recognition of levels and degrees of seriousness of student misbehavior.
2. Some specific remedial actions to be taken, as a matter of course, at each level.
3. Identification of specific personnel to be involved at each step of the disciplinary action process.

Once aspects such as these are identified and delineated, it is relatively easy for the staff to incorporate other essential operational details. These are related to personnel notes, follow-up activities, recordkeeping procedures, and utilization of specialized support people from special service agencies, police, mental health, and welfare, among others.

A suburban middle school used this cooperative approach when the staff wanted to revise and update the building policies in terms of the changing socioeconomic conditions resulting from a sudden large population growth in the community. Parental representation included people who had just moved in as well as those who had been residents of the community for a long period of time. This gave the staff valuable information concerning changing community values and their potential influences on building operation.

Positive results evolved from this series of five cooperative meetings. Several major ones were:

1. New parents became more quickly acquainted with existing community values and school emphases.
2. Staff members became more aware of the school expectations of new residents.
3. Parents were immediately involved in, and supportive of, the school program.

4. New students who were potential problems quickly became aware of the demands and expectations of the school and community through the discussions their parents had with other community residents.

HOW TO: IDENTIFY THE REFERRAL SEQUENCE

The primary reasons for developing a ladder of referral are to provide a sequent order disciplinary action and to clearly identify the involvement of personnel, and their scope of action, at each level. Without this, there is strong tendency for staff members to act in isolation and to take disciplinary actions that are inconsistent with, or in conflict with, actions taken by other teachers. Teachers, also, often tend to feel that they are receiving little, or no, support from other members of the faculty.

An effective referral structure provides a framework that facilitates progressive staff action related to disciplinary measures taken, extent of resource help available, and continuing communication between various staff members dealing with a common behavioral problem. As in any operational framework, however, the effectiveness of the referral structure is determined by how well the teachers function in terms of possibilities available to them.

To facilitate staff action, the referral structure should be developed so that each teacher, parent, and student is aware of the total referral process, who is involved at each level, and the scope of individual staff actions at each level. It is a primary responsibility of each teacher, as the original initiating force, to explain clearly to the students in his classes how he will function within the referral structure. This explanation should include discussion of the extent the teacher will work with a given student to resolve a problem, how the teacher will decide on any needed consequent action, and how he will involve a misbehaving student in these processes.

The referral should also facilitate communication between persons involved. This necessitates the development of record-keeping procedures that are similar at every step of referral. Consistency here helps provide staff members at all levels a detailed record of a given student's behavior pattern, consequent teacher action, and extent of results of these actions. Examples of recordkeeping forms are provided at the end of this chapter, in Figures 10-1 through 10-5.

This continuity in communications is also important from the standpoint of follow-up action. A basic purpose of the referral system is to provide a continuous process for dealing with behavior problems, yet facilitate the solving of the problem at the lowest level possible. If this is to occur, it is essential that staff action at a given level be sequent in terms of the action taken at the previous level. An effective record-keeping system, together with procedures that encourage oral staff information exchange, is vital to the maintenance of staff action continuity.

Time also plays an important role in the communications and referral processes. Middle level students need, and want, time frames of reference. This is especially important in reference to behavior problems. Most middle and junior high youngsters can change their behavior patterns quickly, provided they know specifically the aspects of conduct that are to be changed and are given a time deadline for change. Typically, the time deadline would lengthen as a student is moved from one level of referral to the next. This is necessary because, logically, the further a student is moved up the ladder of referral, the more serious his problem is deemed to be.

HOW TO: DEVELOP REFERRAL LEVEL ONE—
STUDENT AND TEACHER

On a day-to-day basis, most student misbehavior problems should be handled relatively quickly through effective teacher action, at Level One. The referral structure should be designed to facilitate the attainment of rapid solutions in as few referral levels as possible. On the basis, Level One is perhaps the most important step, because misbehavior can be stopped after one incident and because actions at consequent levels are based on teacher actions taken at the first level.

Correctional actions taken by a staff member are aspects of the overall learning program. Consequently, these actions within the referral structure should be consistent with the demands, performance, and functioning patterns expected of the students in the other learning areas. Disciplinary actions, then, must be planned as part of a broader learning plan. This Level One plan, similar in structure at the other levels, would include the following teacher action phases. This similarity in structure enables referral action to be initiated at the level most appropriate to the seriousness of a given act of misbehavior.

When the teacher identifies an act of misconduct, before he takes remedial action he should take time to:

1. Identify causes of misbehavior.
2. Identify the effect of this act on others.
3. Determine the extent this behavior deviates from the students' normal behavior and the conduct expected from this age group.

Once the teacher identifies these causes and effects, he can then make appropriate decisions related to possible actions he can take and the point at which he will act. This involves his determining whether the situation demands discipline or counseling, whether he should place emphasis on developmental or remediation factors, and the specific results he wants to attain.

Before the teacher takes any specific action to solve a discipline problem, he should consider consequent measures he may have to take. Here, a teacher needs to consider how much time he must give a student to change his behavior and the amount of time the teacher is going to devote to working with the student. A point of referral must also be identified. This is the point in time the teacher will refer the student to the next deciplinary level if the problem cannot be satisfactorily resolved at the first level.

Following would be a typical chart of action within the ladder of referral.

Student Misconduct: Student challenged validity of work when asked why he had not completed the assignment. He also challenged the teacher when he said, "If you are going to assign that much work, I'm not going to do it."

Classroom Situation: This student had a past record of erratic class performance. He was capable of doing most of the work. However, if he felt a particular assignment was too difficult, or would take too long to finish, he would not do it. He felt it was up to him since "it was his grade."

Teacher Objective: To have the student develop confidence in accepting challenges and not attempt to blame someone else, and to control his temper.

Time Target: Two to three weeks

Teacher Actions: Possible actions the teacher can take in terms of the misconduct incident include the following:

1. Talking with the student and helping him set personal objectives.
2. Informing the parent of the incident, leaving disciplinary action to the parent (preparation for Level Two referral).
3. Failing the student.
4. Requiring the student to stay after school to make up work.
5. Recommend that the student be moved to a lower level class.
6. Send the student to the assistant principal for disciplinary action (Level Four).

It is at this stage the teacher has to decide which action, or combination of actions, will best facilitate the achievement of his stated objective. The decision the teacher makes here can have a definite effect, positive or negative, on results attained at the next level of referral. Consequently, referral should not be made until the teacher has done all he can to resolve the problem at the student-teacher level. If referral is done too quickly, the student will come to think that he is responsible only to those at the upper referral levels, and not to the teacher as a person.

Referral: This step is taken only when the teacher is convinced other people should be brought into the situation. At this stage, the teacher should be ready to:

1. Identify the specific need for referral.
2. Define the roles and possible actions of the additional people being involved.
3. Reexamine his own actions and stated objectives.
4. Follow up on the actions taken by other people involved.

HOW TO: IMPLEMENT REFFERAL LEVEL TWO—
STUDENT—TEACHER—PARENT

Actions taken at the second level must be identified in terms of the actions taken and extent of results attained at Level One. It is especially important that any actions the parent chooses to take reinforce previous and continuing actions of the teacher. The teacher cannot simply turn the problem over to the parent for solution. Again, it is up to the teacher to develop follow-up measures that will complement parental action. The teacher and the parent, at Level Two, become a team working to solve a problem of mutual concern.

On this basis, it is important that the teacher and parent come to agreement on

1. The identification of the problem and the need for a solution.
2. The roles, responsibilities, and actions of teacher and parent.
3. Methods by which parent and teacher will communicate with each other, and frequency of contact.
4. The results to be attained, and how soon.

The primary purposes of involving the parent are to inform him of his child's performance and to enlist his support in solving a behavioral problem. This is an important level because, in many cases, this is the first level at which the parent is asked to become active in the corrective process involving his child. Careful planning on the part of the teacher is important here because the parent has the opportunity to observe, first-hand, the teacher's methods of operation with the child and with the parent.

If the teacher doesn't clearly define what he expects of the child, the parent, and himself, his effectiveness is going to be limited. It is necessary then for the teacher to follow the procedures outlined for Level One, so that he will have the information needed for delineating his expectations of all three persons involved. Through this approach, the teacher can normally expect the parent to follow through on any consequent misconduct incidents, once he is notified.

One teacher with whom the authors worked was consistent in informing a parent of the problems his child was causing in class. The parent, for a time, was supportive of the teacher and worked to improve his child's behavior. This particular mother, however, became rather frustrated after a period of time because the teacher gave different reasons for the child's misbehavior each time the parent and teacher conferred. The parent felt there was no continuity in the complaints and was confused about what was expected of her. Had the teacher kept a progressive record of the incidents, causes, objectives, and consequent actions, he would have been aware of any behavioral pattern developing. He would, then, have been able to provide more consistent guidance for the parent.

As more people become involved, it becomes more important for the teacher to collect information. This information will be used in different ways, depending upon the role each person is expected to assume in working with a problem. The success these people will have in supporting the teacher's efforts will be dependent on the assistance the teacher gives them through his recordkeeping and his own efforts to resolve a conflict.

HOW TO: CONTROL THROUGH REFERRAL LEVEL THREE—
STUDENT—TEACHER—PARENT—COUNSELOR

This is the first level in which a support person is involved to any direct extent. Since the counselor becomes involved on the basis of the teacher's decision to refer a student problem to Level Three, it is incumbent on the teacher to see his role as a team member with the counselor and parent, and yet retain the position as team leader. He should not turn the problem over to the counselor and then withdraw. It is still the teacher's responsibility to implement procedures developed by the teacher-counselor team.

The counselor should be involved when the teacher and parent feel a problem evidenced by misbehavior indicates a need for counseling rather than more formal discipline approaches. This decision commits the teacher to a delay in administering punishment for unacceptable actions by the student. The teacher assumes more of a role of implementation because he is putting into effect behavioral demands developed in a teacher-counselor-parent team situation.

A primary objective of the team functioning at Level Three is to identify causal factors generating specific misbehavior. One of the most effective approaches here is the "staffing technique." This involves the scheduling of conferences on a need basis in which all staff members who have some direct responsibility for the pupil in question discuss their experiences with the child, methods they have used, and the consequent results. From the information gained here, a plan of remedial action can be developed.

Another approach that can be used at this level is for the counselor to take primary charge of the student, keeping him out of several sessions of class. During this time, the counselor and student attempt to determine causes and effects of the student's negative conduct. After these have been identified, the counselor, student, teacher, and parent meet together to develop a cooperative plan of action in which each person's responsibilities are carefully defined.

In one metropolitan middle level school, these two methods were used so successfully that individual teacher-counselor teams were teamed on a continuing basis. The teacher would identify a particular class that had potential problem students in it. On a regular basis, the counselor would visit the class simply as an observer. At other times, the counselor would assume various instructional responsibilities and the teacher would observe.

Through this approach, both staff members were able to recognize situations that prompted misconduct and student actions that preceded it. As a result, the team was able to identify situations and problems that were beginning to develop and to deal with them on a preventive basis before they became serious. At various times, all counselors in the school became involved in this.

At Level Three it is important that the continued involvement of the parent is stressed. The teacher and counselor must be aware of the need to work closely with the parent on a continuing basis. Inconsistency in parental influence can have a negative effect on both teacher and counselor efforts.

Following is an example of the ways roles and responsibilities can be delineated.

Problem: Consistent rudeness to teacher and other adults who student feels are "trying to order him around." Makes uncomplimentary remarks about the teacher to other students during class.

Classroom Situation: These incidents occur usually when the student is given a specific task to do and a deadline for completing it. He is especially vocal when work assignments are to be handed in before the end of the class period.

POSSIBLE ACTIONS:

Teacher	Counselor	Parent
1. Isolate student.	1. Call a "staffing" conference.	1. Develop a schedule of home chores and days of week these are to be done.
2. Set deadline in cooperation with student.	2. Help student identify reasons for his actions.	
3. Allow him to make his statement to entire class and let them respond to him.	3. Develop a student self-improvement contract.	2. Keep a log of parent student conflicts and reasons for these.
4. Keep a running log of incidents and discuss these with the student.	4. In a series of counseling sessions, give tasks and deadlines.	3. Keep a record of how many times child is told to do something and number of deadline extensions.
	5. Have student keep his own log of incidents and suggested ways of how he would rather have directions given.	

After the teacher, counselor, and parent have completed their tasks, they can compare results and develop a sequent plan of action based on individual successes they have had in working with the child. The student should be permitted to attend this assessment conference and participate in the making of decisions. In this way, he is, on a progressive basis, committing himself to improving his conduct.

HOW TO: DEVELOP REFERRAL LEVEL FOUR— ASSISTANT PRINCIPAL–STUDENT–PARENT

Referral Level Four is the first step in which a school administrator becomes formally involved in a disciplinary situation. With this involvement, staff members working at the lower referral levels have indicated that more drastic action is needed to resolve a particular case.

Action at this level needs to be taken in terms of a time line and specific deadlines so that the offending student can, as quickly as possible, develop a behavior pattern that is not offensive to staff members and other students. Measures taken at this level must be based on progressive actions taken at the previous levels. These measures must be more demanding of the student in terms of what is expected of him if he is to respect the school's behavior code. Lack of effective action at the administrative level contributes to the feeling on the part of other staff members and students that staff behavior demands mean little. Referral, then, is just a procedure for shifting the responsibility from one person to another.

By the time a behavior problem has reached the fourth level, usually the offending student has developed a negative behavior pattern and he actively resists any attempts to change his conduct. The administrator here, then, must be concerned with developing a pattern-change process. The procedures he uses, of necessity, involve the teacher and parent. It is not always necessary for the counselor to be included.

At this level, there are three major approaches the assistant principal can utilize: (1) use of support referral agencies, (2) variation of class schedule, and (3) parent-student contracting. These can be used separately or in combination.

Support Referral Agencies: Generally such agencies as mental health clinics, medical clinics, and schools for students with emotional problems are involved when the school staff perceives a discipline situation as a symptom of deeper problems. Once these agencies become involved the school personnel assume a secondary role. They implement procedures and approaches suggested by the referral specialists. The teachers do, however, work closely with the agency personnel in evaluating results and developing follow-up procedures when the student returns to the school program.

Class Schedule Variations: Schedule variation can be used as a means of keeping a student in school part time while he is working with a referral agency. This can also be an effective technique for the administrator to use when he and other staff members are dealing with a student who poses a problem in just one or two classes. The schedule variation approach provides the assistant principal with a high degree of flexibility as he works to change the negative behavior of a student.

Perhaps the class schedule variation that would be used most often is the removal of a student from a class in which he is causing trouble, and reassigning him to a class in which functioning demands and teacher operational patterns are different. This changing of a single class usually is effective when misconduct is attributed to a student's being in the same class with members of his peer clique, when he can assume a leadership role in the class, or when he realizes a particular teacher cannot control him. Generally, in this case, misbehavior is identified as being a result of a student grouping situation, and poor conduct is of short duration.

In situations where a student's negative conduct is over a prolonged period of time and support personnel outside the school staff must be involved, the placing of the student on a short schedule can be effective. To place a student on a modified schedule, the school administrator would permit the student to attend classes in which he is not a disturbing influence and take him out of the classes in which he causes trouble.

During the time he is withheld from classes, the student would be scheduled with personnel such as counselors, psychologists, parole officers, or one of the administrators. In instances when the pupil was scheduled to meet with support specialists in the evenings, along with his parents, the student could be taken home by his parents during the time he was not permitted to attend class. The student would not be put back on the school schedule until he could return to all the classes from which he was taken.

A third approach is the use of the progressive schedule variation. Here, the student is taken out of the classes in which he causes disturbances, but is returned to each class as soon as he has shown the capability and desire to maintain conduct deemed acceptable in the class. The progressive approach takes into consideration that, in many instances, corrective efforts take longer for one class situation than another. The student is given immediate recognition for progress in conduct improvement when he is readmitted to one class. This recognition often encourages the student to work to get back into his other classes. Student recognition of success is a key to self-improvement.

HOW TO: IMPLEMENT REFERRAL LEVEL FIVE—
PRINCIPAL—ASSISTANT PRINCIPAL—PARENT—STUDENT

A discipline problem is referred to the fifth level when the offending student resists all efforts to improve his behavior and actively persists in maintaining his disruptive pattern of action. At this stage, negative behavior is generally looked upon as being habitual. There is need for drastic action to resolve the problem. Decisions made by the school administrators are predicated on the belief that all actions possible to resolve a discipline situation have been taken at the previous levels.

With this in mind, the principal and assistant principal have several options available to them.

1. Require the student and his parents to work with a referral agency.
2. Exclude the student from school until, through a series of conferences between family and school, he shows improvement in student conduct.
3. Recommend student for expulsion.
4. Work with parents to have student enrolled in another school.

In requiring the student to work with a referral agency, the school administration is, in effect, saying that the problem is beyond the capabilities of school personnel and that the only way to resolve the situation is to engage parents and student in family counseling. This involves a formal evaluation of the family situation and its carry-over effect in the school environment. This formal assessment approach goes beyond the Level Four referral step, which usually only involves the student working with a social worker or psychologist at the school.

Upon the recommendation of the referral personnel, the administrators may reinstate the student in school on a modified schedule, or they may suspend the student entirely until the referral specialist recommends the student to be returned to his classes. It is important that the principal and assistant principal obtain this recommendation to avoid any conflict with the parents over the student's being prevented from attending school. Many parents will hesitate before actively resisting this type of professional recommendation.

The school administrators may decide to exclude a student from school while they work with the parents for a period of time. Exclusion is different from expulsion in that the student is prevented from attending class for an indefinite time, usually a period of from four to ten days. During this time, the parents, student, and school personnel work together to identify the student's problems and ways they can work as a team to improve the pupil's behavior. In this situation, a specialist from a referral agency may be involved as a team member if the parents and/or principals deem it advisable.

Level Five is the only stage at which a student can be recommended for expulsion for two reasons. First, this is normally the first level in which the principal becomes actively involved and he is the only building level staff member who can make the recommendation. Second, before this level, not enough pertinent information can be gathered together in terms of a student's persistence in refusing to perform in an acceptable manner and the staff's doing all within its capabilities to help him.

Expulsion is the last resort of the school, and separates the child completely from the school setting usually for the remainder of the school term. As a result, along with the suggestion for expulsion, the school staff should recommend alternative education pursuits for the child for the period of time he is out of his classes. These alternatives should be identified in terms of the child's problems and in terms of his adjustment when he returns to school.

Among alternative possibilities the school staff may recommend are:

1. Assignment of a home-bound teacher.
2. Volunteer tutoring in the home or some other off-campus location.
3. Identification of specific objectives related to conduct that the student, and his parents, can work to achieve during the time he is out of school.
4. Selected staff members and referral agency personnel working with the child on a regular appointment basis. School staff involvement here would be to help the child maintain informal contact with the school.

The fourth option available to the school staff is their working to have the child enrolled in another school. This action would be predicated on the belief that a major change in school environment, peer associates, and teacher functioning demands could help the student. The child's attendance at another school would be contingent upon his overt actions. If he made a satisfactory adjustment, he could remain at that school until he was ready to enter high school. If his conduct were still unsatisfactory, he would be recommended for expulsion.

The success of this transfer approach is dependent upon the extent to which the faculty of the receiving school is willing to work with the youngster. This is a calculated risk because the child's reputation usually precedes him to the school. It has been the author's experience, however, that if the student's new instructors are selected in terms of their capabilities to work with problem children, the child usually is able to remain in school.

Follow up procedures at Level Five, as at the other levels, are important, for a student's change in behavior will be temporary unless positive staff reinforcement actions are maintained. These follow-up actions will be determined by the administrative decision related to the child's reinstatement in school.

1. Once reinstated, misbehavior action begins again at Level One.
2. Once reinstated, actions at Level Five are initiated.

A decision here is going to be made in terms of any success the staff has had in working with the student and in terms of the seriousness of the student's misbehavior following his readmission to his classes. A thorough review of the student's anecdotal record should be performed before this decision is made. An incorrect decision can cause more staff problems by giving the offending pupil added opportunities to disrupt classes, or it can negatively affect the child by depriving him of additional help from which he may possibly benefit. Careful following of the complete ladder-of-referral can help the staff make the correct decision.

DISCIPLINE RECORDKEEPING FORMS

The following are five examples of discipline recordkeeping forms used at different levels of the ladder of referral at Goddard Middle School, Littleton, Colorado.

TEACHER–
STUDENT DISCIPLINE JOURNAL

DATE	STUDENT	INFRACTION	PENALTY	INITIAL	
					A*
					B
					C
					D
					E
					F
					G
					H
					I
					J
					K
					L
					M
					N
					O
					P
					Q
					R
					S
					T
					U
					V
					W
					X
					Y
					Z

*Alphabetical List Finder

Figure 10-1
Referral Level One—Student and Teacher

GODDARD MIDDLE SCHOOL

Littleton, Colorado

Date

Dear Parents:

This is to notify you that _____

_____ is to be commended for his/her school work to date.

_____ is working below his/her ability at this time.

_____ is doing unsatisfactory work at this time.

The factors checked below are important. They will give you considerable insight into the progress of your child at this time in _____.

	Good	Improvement Needed	Unsatisfactory (Reason for Failure)
Interest in learning			
Study habits			
Completion of assignments			
Completion of make-up assignments.			
Test performance			
Follows directions			
Brings materials to class			
Participation in class			
Use of school time			
Requests extra help			
Respects rules and regulations			
Cooperation			
Attention in class			
Class attendance			
Behavior			
Assumption of responsibility			
Social adjustment			

Comments: _____

If the school may be of assistance, please contact either the teacher or the counselor. Please call the school secretary, 798-2563, to make an appointment for your conference; otherwise, the teacher or counselor may be committed to other meetings.

(Copy included in student's cumulative record)

PARENT COPY   Teacher

Figure 10-2
Referral Level Two——Student—Parent—Teacher

Goddard School
Littleton, Colorado

Progress Report

Student Name _____ Subject _____ Grade 5 6 7 8 9

Teacher _____ Date _____ Estimated Grade Average _____

STRENGTH IN ACADEMIC WORK

1. ___ Contributions to class discussion
2. ___ Does more work than required
3. ___ Seems to work to capacity
4. ___ Organizes work well
5. ___ Grasps major ideas
6. ___ Reads well
7. ___ Accurate in work
8. ___ Has original ideas
9. ___ Punctual in work
10. ___ Willing worker
11. ___ Papers always near

WEAKNESS

1. ___ Irregular attendance
2. ___ Assignments are not in on time
3. ___ Tired or drowsy in class
4. ___ Class recitation poor
5. ___ Tests low or failing
6. ___ Does not master subject matter
7. ___ Inability to read directions
8. ___ Does not come with books & working material
9. ___ Inattentive in class
10. ___ Works too slowly
11. ___ Does just enough to get by on assignments
12. ___ Does not follow directions
13. ___ Work carelessly done
14. ___ Too many outside activities
15. ___ Wastes time

SOCIAL DEVELOPMENT

1. ___ Courteous–Considerate
2. ___ Shows leadership
3. ___ Wants too much attention
4. ___ Seems less grown-up than average
5. ___ Has many friends
6. ___ Shy
7. ___ Satisfactory
8. ___ Should show more respect to fellow students
9. ___ Should show more respect at extra-curricular activities such as Student Assemblies, Field Trips and Ball Games
10. ___ Prefers to work individually
11. ___ Seems more grown-up than average
12. ___ Works best in group

PLANS OR SUGGESTIONS FOR IMPROVEMENT

_____
_____
_____

COOPERATION WITH CLASSROOM RULES

1. ___ Doesn't show proper respect for property
2. ___ Frequently needs to be reminded of rules
3. ___ Does not respect rules and authority
4. ___ Does respect rules and authority
5. ___ Bothers other students
6. ___ Volunteers for extra work
7. ___ Shows improvement

REQUESTED BY:

Parents _____ Principal _____
Teacher _____ Counselor _____ Counselor: _____

Figure 10-3
Referral Level Three——Counselor—Teacher—Parent—Student

```
┌─────────────────────────────────────────────────────────────┐
│                    GODDARD SCHOOL                             │
│                    Littleton, Colorado                        │
│                                                               │
│                                    DUE DATE _____       │
│                                                               │
│   STUDENT: _____   DATE _____          │
│                                                               │
│   TEACHER _____   SUBJECT: _____         │
│                                                               │
│   ESTIMATED GRADE: _____ REASON FOR REPORT: _____        │
│                                                               │
│                                   _____      │
│                                                               │
│                                   _____      │
│                                                               │
│   COMMENTS:                                                   │
│                                                               │
└─────────────────────────────────────────────────────────────┘
```

Figure 10-4
Referral Level Three──Counselor─Teacher─Parent─Student
(Can be used as an optional teacher-counselor referral form.)

GODDARD SCHOOL
3800 West Berry Avenue
798-2563

DISCIPLINE REFERRAL

STUDENT NAME	TELEPHONE	GRADE	DATE	TIME

REFERRED BY _____

DESCRIBE INCIDENT:

HAS THIS OR SIMILAR BEHAVIOR OCCURRED BEFORE?	INDICATE CORRECTIVE STEPS TAKEN TO DATE:
( ) YES ( ) NO	( ) WARNINGS AND LECTURES (APPROX. NUM.) _____
	( ) DETENTIONS (APPROX. AMOUNT OF TIME) _____
	( ) PARENT CONTACT
	( ) COUNSELOR CONTACT
HOW MANY TIMES? _____	( ) OTHER _____
	( ) NONE

STUDENT STATEMENT:

ACTION TAKEN: (FOR OFFICE USE)	REMARKS:
( ) CONFERENCE WITH STUDENT	
( ) DETENTION _____ HOUR(S)	
( ) APOLOGY REQUIRED TO _____	
( ) PARENT PHONE CONTACT	
( ) LETTER SENT HOME	
( ) COPY OF REFERRAL SENT HOME	
( ) PARENT CONFERENCE	
( ) REFERRED TO COUNSELOR	
( ) SUSPENSION OF _____ DAYS	
( ) ISOLATION OF ____ DAYS	
( ) OTHER:	

_____
ASSISTANT PRINCIPAL

CC: ( ) REFERRAL TEACHER   ( ) PARENT   ( ) ASSISTANT SUPERINTENDENT   ( ) COUNSELOR   ( ) FILE   ( ) OTHER _____

Figure 10-5
Referral Levels Four and Five——Principal—
Assistant Principal—Parent—Student

Conclusion

Our readers should note that time and time again the authors indicate the importance of specific techniques or routines in handling the majority of school discipline problems. It would initially seem that by implying we have and use techniques or routines that this would destroy the individualistic approach which is so necessary in helping young people work through their problems. However, technique implies a considerable degree of forethought, which gives to the experienced administrator, teacher, or parent a multifaceted instantaneous catalog of workable ways of handling varying types of disciplinary cases. This means that we do develop and do follow patterns of tried disciplinary techniques which we find to be successful in working in our individual school setting.

THE RIGHT PERSON FOR THE RIGHT JOB

Communities have an obligation to seek out qualified administrators and teachers to be in charge of and work with school discipline. Fortunate is the community and school system which, before hiring potential administrators and teachers, readily identifies its personnel needs in terms of basic philosophies. This facet of preparatory involvement is one of the most vital factors related to the final success of school personnel that a school or community must accept. Many teachers and administrators are doomed to failure, even before they are on the job, just because of the hurry-up factor in hiring practices. Potential personnel must know what the school system and community wants, and what kinds of problems they will face. Philosophies are as different as are humans, and it takes time to bring together a winning combination of the two.

Once the philosophies have been readily agreed upon by community and school personnel, the usual hiring procedures can be followed without difficulty. A district should hire only those persons whose qualifications, both academically and personally, fit all of the established requirements. Such personal traits as maturity, personality, age, and sex can affect the final success of the people who are in charge of disciplinary procedures.

It should also be noted that although some teachers and administrators, and their techniques, work successfully in some communities, the same people might not be successful working in other communities.

ADMINISTRATIVE TECHNIQUE

Once a school has hired an administrative person to be in charge of student discipline, it is important that teachers and parents understand the procedures that are to be used in handling discipline problems. These practices and procedures should be openly discussed within the faculty, and also by parents and students. Teachers should be comfortable in the knowledge that when they seek help, they will receive help in handling discipline problems. It is also important for the faculty to understand that to ask for help in solving such problems does not imply a personal weakness or lack of ability on the part of the teacher. We cannot be all things to all people, although some teachers and administrators might come closer to fulfilling this statement than others. Teachers must understand that it is just as much a crime to allow a class to be continually disrupted by a few as it is to not be able to admit that there is a problem taking place. Offenders, no matter what their number, should not be allowed to handicap a program which is aimed at helping all of the students in a class setting, and those offenders should be set aside temporarily so that the majority might benefit.

PARENT INVOLVEMENT

Parents must accept equal responsibility in helping solve their childrens' discipline problems. Unfortunately, many parents are so involved emotionally with their children that they cease to function positively when the discipline environment demands consistency and sternness. It is not uncommon in this day and age to find parents who, even with ten to fourteen-year-olds, have given up completely with regard to discipline, manners, and so on. This type of parent needs as much help, if not more, than their children.

Another rather startling revelation relates to a complete lack of understanding on the part of some parents concerning their understanding of child psychology, child growth patterns, and discipline. Being a parent does not automatically imply a certain degree of common sense and wisdom. Wisdom comes through experience and learning daily from one's mistakes. The majority of parents, fortunately, raise beautiful, well-disciplined children; however, some parents, unfortunately, are *used* by their children. When this is the case there is little hope, at least temporarily, of solving a young person's problems.

Parents, like teachers and school administrators, must work closely together with school and community personnel to solve young peoples' problems. No one group can do the job alone. If there is an inconsistency in group handling techniques or philosophy which allows for a child to pit one group against another, the child is the one who will be hurt in the long run, for this teaches him that it is possible to manipulate people in a negative manner. If this happens enough times, selfish traits become rooted very deeply, and eventually that individual's personality accepts those traits as being normal types of behavioral interaction.

PSYCHOLOGICAL AND PSYCHIATRIC SERVICES

Even though the majority of school personnel and parents can and do work closely together, it sometimes behooves the school and parents to reach for professional psychological and/or psychiatric help. The slogan, "The sooner a problem can be identified and probable solutions decided upon, the sooner a cure will be achieved," is very apropos when it comes to working with young people. As has been stated many times, discipline problems can be the resultant reaction emanating from many causes. However, one should also keep in mind that such problems might stem from nothing more than a lack of maturity on the part of the student. When this is the case, much damage can take place if the student is forced into unnecessary psychological testing programs, which usually have follow-up psychological and/or psychiatric services.

A HANDBOOK

The primary objective of this book is to present alternatives in disciplinary procedures which school personnel and parents can use in helping young people work through those problems which eventually become discipline cases. As a handbook, parents can readily refer to it for an understanding of why school personnel use such techniques, and also why at times, school personnel run out of answers. The handbook approach will give to all members of a school system a myriad of approaches to disciplinary procedure and, in turn, recommend to the reader how these approaches can be adapted to many environments. The handbook should also help bring an awareness to the community of the value and need for well-thought-out discipline routines which point out the fact that discipline is really a total community effort and not just the responsibility of school or home.

Index

Index